The Sacred Texts

The Sacred Texts

Mandukya Upanishad and Isha Upanishad

Kathiresan Ramachanderam

PARTRIDGE
A Penguin Random House Company

To order additional copies of this book, contact
Partridge India
000 800 10062 62
orders.india@partridgepublishing.com

www.partridgepublishing.com/india

Contents

Prologue

I write this at a time when Hawk's Nest is besieged by enemies that have boldly and brazenly invaded its territories on all permissible fronts. These enemies have little care or concern for our cherished time-honored way of life and I fear that the knowledge that we have accumulated over the ages might be gradually eroded and mortals might be swayed by the cohesive and persuasive powers of the Dark Lord and consent to accepting the infernal child of darkness as their sovereign liege and Lord Protector. It is therefore imperative to codify our teachings and condense them into volumes so that posterity may read and decipher its contents and mortality may not totally succumb to the to the blasphemous powers of darkness. I call these volumes the Sacred Texts.

In order for any text to be granted or conferred the designation "sacred text" the text must fulfill certain criteria. The narrative must fulfill six salient conditions. The requirements are that the selected text elaborates on the creation of the universe (sarga), the periodical process of destruction and re-creation (pratisaryga), the various eras (manvantara), the history of the Solar Dynasty (Surya Vamsha), the history of the Lunar Dynasty (Chandra Vamsha) and the royal genealogies (vamshanucharita).

The mode of worship prescribed differs in many aspects to contemporary norms. It is foreseeable, given the current state of affairs, that our age old rites and rituals will gradually be eroded by the passage of time.

The sacred texts are written in order to bring us closer to the super-soul or the super-consciousness, the Brahmatma and the fourth dimension. The Brahmatma is the sole singular entity from which all things animate and inanimate emanate. He is the past, the present and the future and realization of the Brahmatma allows us to breach the space time continuum. Space travel, time travel, inter-dimensional travel, inter-spherical travel and all things improbable become possible when we achieve cognizance and realize the singular truth.

In the beginning there was only the single entity that which is known as the Brahmatma; the super consciousness or the collective consciousness. The super soul is colorless, odorless, genderless, formless, shapeless and all prevailing. The Brahmatma is both matter and antimatter and it is both existence and non-existence.

Then there was a division, the Brahmatma split into two parts representing the opposing forces that manipulate the universe, the positive aspect of the Brahmatma and the negative aspect of the Brahmatma. The opposing forces further collided and in the ensuing explosion the powers of the Brahmatma were vested in three different entities, Brahma, Vishnu and Shiva. All good and evil, in the present universe, stem or emanate from the Trinity.

Each of these entities further subdivided into two distinct entities, the former male and the latter female to enable procreation and continuation. The division of the Brahmatma occurs at the start of each universal cycle and it is symbolic of new beginnings.

The division of the super-soul endures for eight point six four-billion-years before it contracts and retracts and the source or the central nexus which links all things in every universal cycle is the super-consciousness, a warehouse that stores all information i.e. all that has happened and all that will happen in the eight point six four-billion-years of each universal cycle. This mammoth storage facility or vast collective warehouse is known as the fourth dimension.

The universe in reality endures for one day of Brahma (the personification of the creative faculties of the Brahmatma) which is equivalent to eight point six four-billion-years and in religious circles one Brahmanic day is known as a Kalpa. In each Kalpa there are fourteen Manvantras and for each Manvantra there is one Manu. The universe ends and recreates itself at the end of each Kalpa or at the end of the fourteenth Manvantras. In each Manvantra there are Seven Great Saptarishis or Great Sages born from the creative powers of the Brahmatma or the super-soul. They are as follows: -

- ❖ Bharadvaja
- ❖ Gautama
- ❖ Atri
- ❖ Jamadagni
- ❖ Kashyapa
- ❖ Vasishta
- ❖ Vishvamitra

The Gods, the Saptarishis, the creative aspect of the Brahmatma (Brahma) and he who holds the title Indra re-appears without fail in each Manvantara. In each Manvantara, there is a Manu or an overlord. The names of the fourteen Manus that preside over each Manvantra are as follows: -

- ❖ 1st Manvantra - Svayambhuva Manu
- ❖ 2nd Manvantra - Svarochisha Manu
- ❖ 3rd Manvantra - Outtama Manu
- ❖ 4th Manvantra - Tamas Manu
- ❖ 5th Manvantra - Raivata Manu
- ❖ 6th Manvantra - Chakshusha Manu
- ❖ 7th Manvantra - Vaivasvata Manu
- ❖ 8th Manvantra - Savarni Manu
- ❖ 9th Manvantra - Rouchya Manu
- ❖ 10th Manvantra - Bhoutya Manu
- ❖ 11th Manvantra - Merusavarni Manu
- ❖ 12th Manvantra - Rita Manu
- ❖ 13th Manvantra - Ritadhama Manu
- ❖ 14th Manvantra - Vishvakasena Manu

I write this during the reign of Vaivasvata Manu or the seventh overlord, in the seventh Manvantara. Six Manvantara's have gone by and there are seven more to come.

At the start of each universal cycle there is an explosion that compels an expansion or expulsion outwards and the universe continues to expand in this manner to this very day. It is therefore crucial to acknowledge and understand that all things known and unknown, created and uncreated, procreated and un-procreated start at the same point. There is only one source to all things and that source is the Brahmatma.

All things animate and inanimate contain within their material composition a minute component of the Brahmatma which is best described as a tiny white light, the size of a thumb and it is this tiny white light that gives all things substance. This tiny white light is called the farvashi or the soul and the farvashi of all things is an integral component of the super-soul or in other words an infinitesimal component of the Brahmatma.

The distinction between the soul and the body can be made in the following manner: - the soul is energy and the body, matter. Energy cannot be created or destroyed but it can change from one form to another. Thus an untainted soul can be tainted and the reverse can also occur. Energy can also be transferred from one object to another and thus the spirit that has remained can occupy the body of another. Matter is best defined as any object that has mass and takes up space. Matter is finite, energy is infinite.

The purpose of mortality or restricting or confining the soul to a mortal body is for the soul to gain awareness or to achieve cognizance of the Brahmatma and for the mortal body through the prescribed avenue of transcendental sleep or meditative sleep to be in union with the super-soul.

Once the connection is made and the melding is complete the soul shares the knowledge of the Brahmatma, which in reality includes the memories and the recollections of the entire universe, past present and future.

Those who are born with the link to the Brahmatma intact, un-tampered and un-fettered by conscious desires are classed or categorized as mortals with the gift of the talent. Under normal circumstance this sharing of knowledge only occurs while the physical body is in a state of temporary abeyance or in a state of self-imposed paralysis. The mind via the link to the super-consciousness can travel to any location in the universe and the term that is used to refer to this mode of travel is astral projection. When a mortal is in a deep meditative state, he or she is actuality transgressing and traversing the present universe.

That however is not the case with those that are born with the talent intact for their actions are not directed by the conscious mind or the physical mind but by the soulful mind or the subconscious mind which is linked directly to the super-consciousness. Therefore, for them there is no need to go into transcendental sleep or to slow the consciousness down through the prescribed mode of meditation.

In our cosmology the universe is part of an endless cycle of creation, destruction and regeneration. Each cycle lasts for a period of eight point six four-billion-years. The universe begins, expands and contracts in lots of eight point six four-billion-years but the Brahmatma the sole and single source of all beginnings and endings lasts forever. The term forever doesn't mean an eternity or for all creation because both "an eternity" and "all creation" are measurable and quantifiable allotments of time i.e. eight point six four-billion-years.

Forever simply means that which is beyond measure or beyond mortal comprehension or that which is beyond creation and destruction.

As for the soul it remains forever but in many instances it is encased in a mortal body. The duration of each soul as a separate entity even if it was subjected to repeated and endless reincarnations is at worst or at best a mere eight point six four-billion-years.

Existence as we know it endures for a period of four point three-two-million years which is divided into four stages. The first stage is called Satya Yuga and it extends for a period of one point seven-two-eight million years. Satya Yuga is referred to as the age of enlightenment and all mortals born during this age are single minded in their intent, purpose and willingness to be united with the Brahmatma.

The sole purpose of birth during this era is to be at one with the super-soul. It is the golden age of our scriptures, the Vedas and Vedic teachings take preference over all other matters.

Satya Yuga begins on the seventh day of Vaishakh Shukla Tritiya, also known as Akshaya Tritiya. The positive aspect of the Brahmatma graces the mortal world at four different intervals in the form of Matsya (the fish), Koorma (the tortoise), Varaha (the boar) and Narasimha (he who is part man and part lion) during this period. Knowledge, meditation and transcendental sleep hold special significance and importance during Satya Yuga.

The golden age is followed by three other stages and as humanity progresses from one stage to another the impact of the Vedas, the dissemination of Vedic teachings and its applications gradually decline and towards the end, Vedic teachings are superseded by material and temporal pursuits.

Satya Yuga is followed by Treta Yuga which lasts for a period of one point two-nine-six million years. The positive aspect of the Brahmatma descends upon the earth in the form of Vamana and Parashurama.

Corporeal pursuits decrease and diminish towards the end of Treta Yuga and the onset of Dvapara Yuga which lasts for eight hundred and sixty-four thousand years. The positive aspect of the Brahmatma returns to mortal world in the form of Rama and Krishna.

Dvapara Yuga is followed by Kali Yuga the final stage before destruction and regeneration and it lasts for a period of four hundred and thirty-two-thousand years. During Kali Yuga the positive aspect of the Brahmatma descends upon the earth in the form of Buddha and Kalki.

Vedic teachings are at the lowest ebb during Kali Yuga and it culminates in an epic battle following which Satya Yuga begins again. Mortality endures for the length of the universe and the mortal world exists in four point three-two-million year cycles. The soul exists forever and the length of time that it exists for is both immeasurable and unquantifiable.

The first text the Mandukya Upanishad paves the way for mortality to reach out and to link with the super-consciousness and despite the trials and tribulations that accompany existence at the time of Kali Yuga; it is still possible to construct the bridge with the super-soul.

It is first and foremost a recognition of the Brahmatma and puts us on a path through which we can further explore the knowledge that is stored in the unlimited warehouse that is called the super-consciousness.

It is also relevant at this stage to elaborate on the human mind and the component or the aspect of the mind that is constantly in touch with the super-consciousness or the Brahmatma.

The mind is divided into two components the conscious mind or the reactive mind (so called because it reacts to urges, cravings and impulses. It is also called the temporal mind because it is constantly preoccupied with worldly affairs) and the subconscious mind or the component or the aspect of the mind that is always in abeyance i.e. it never comes to life unless the conscious mind is at rest which only happens or occurs during sleep or temporary paralysis.

During the day the physical body is active and the conscious mind comes to the forefront, while the subconscious mind is in a state of abeyance. To a large degree the subconscious mind is suppressed by the conscious mind.

It is only when the conscious mind goes to rest during sleep, natural or induced or the body is in a state of temporary paralysis for example due to an unforeseen illness or an accident, that the subconscious mind which in reality is the part of the mind that is linked to the super-consciousness swings into action.

The human body is divided into two components, the physical body and the soul, which is a light no bigger than the size of a thumb. The conscious mind belongs to the physical body and the subconscious mind belongs to the soul.

The conscious mind is constantly and consistently preoccupied with activities that permeate the physical body and the subconscious mind is constantly preoccupied with the activities that nourish the soul but because of the limitations that are imposed on the soul when it is encased or trapped within the confines of the physical body only one component of the body can function at a time.

In the case of those blessed with the talent however the situation is different and their actions are constantly and consistently directed by the subconscious mind.

During the day, during the hours when the physical body is awake, the conscious mind is preoccupied with satisfying the needs of the senses, propelled and compelled by the desire to gratify sensual urges and it is never satisfied or fulfilled until and unless it has achieved the rewards that it so desires.

At this time the subconscious mind of most mortals can do little but lurk behind hidden corners or stalk the numerous labyrinths of the mind and its presence is often unfelt.

During sleep or temporary paralysis either natural or induced, the subconscious mind springs to life, freed from the shackles of the conscious mind. It is also the time when the physical body is subjected to dreams. There are in reality four categories of dreams. The normal dream that which is inconsequential and insubstantial, the gift dream, the outer body experience and the regressive dream.

The normal dream can be dismissed as flashes of a mortal's experiences, hopes, fears, aspirations, inspirations and ambitions. It has no impact on daily existence.

The second category of dreams are gift dreams, so called simply because it is a gift to be able to experience these dreams. Gift dreams can be induced or adduced by achieving or acquiring a closer nexus with the Brahmatma. In reality these dreams are a mechanism through which the subconscious mind makes the physical body aware of the future.

Clairvoyant dreams fall into the category of gift dreams. These are dreams that foretell the future and are indicative of an event in a mortal's life that is about to unfold and at times the mortal is made aware of a future outcome be it either positive or negative. It is more prevalent in those that have greater physic abilities than others. Physic abilities are at times genetic or are abilities that have been handed down the line.

The "gift dream" can also be induced via hypnosis and stimulated by meditation. In either state the conscious mind is temporarily put to sleep.

In the former the subconscious mind makes an explosive entry or an entry without notice and the subject is instantly preoccupied with the memories, thoughts and recollections of the other. In the latter the subconscious mind makes an informal gradual entry and the subject slowly begins to understand the subtle nuances of the subconscious mind.

In the former the subject is unable to recall what he or she had said while under the influence of a hypnotist while in the latter the subject is able to recollect all that he or she had experienced while in the meditative state.

Physic abilities also include telekinesis i.e. the ability to move objects with thought or at higher levels alter the composition of matter. I must caution however that it is also possible to attain these abilities through the aid and assistance of spirits.

We have to constantly keep in mind that the Brahmatma is both positive and negative i.e. all good emanates from the Brahmatma as does all evil and the universe is at equilibrium when good and evil are balanced.

There is a constant perpetual struggle between both aspects or manifestations of the Brahmatma and this struggle will continue for eight point six four-billion-years and towards the end good and evil will negate each other and in the process destroy the universe, wiping the slate clean and paving the way for a new cycle to begin.

The outer body experience is a result of sharing the positive qualities of the Brahmatma and during the dream the subject feels himself lifted and flung thousands if not millions or billions of miles from his body and experiences and senses pleasures and objects in surroundings that he or she is unfamiliar with and sometimes is unable to identify with. The consciousness of the Brahmatma is limitless and there is no telling what the subject may experience.

Likewise, the regressive dream is also the result of sharing the consciousness of the Brahmatma but as opposed to the outer body experience where the subject feels himself drifting higher and higher towards the clouds, in these dreams the subject experiences a falling sensation as he falls lower and lower spiraling down into an abyss. In most instances those who experience these types of dreams are able to talk and commune with the dead.

It is also relevant at this stage to examine more closely the near death experience that most shamans (as in the case of the Dron Shamans of the Betan Plateau) experience prior to acquiring the abilities that are essential to attaining shaman-hood.

With the erosion and devolution of our teachings and the overwhelming influences of the Dark Lord the practice of shamanism has become increasingly more prevalent and I feel that it is only appropriate that I touch on it, briefly at least, for us to acquire a greater understanding of Shamanism and grasp its fundamentals so we know exactly what we are dealing with.

I fear that should our religious order falter and collapse than shamanism will feature more prominently in the lives of those who inhabit or occupy our present territories and parts of the former Grand Empire.

According to the near death experience theory which is more or less a principle of shaman-hood, the shaman must have crossed the life-death threshold at least momentarily prior to becoming a shaman i.e. he or she must have died for at least a second before being brought back to life or regaining consciousness.

When the prospective shaman crosses the life-death threshold, the soul for a split second leaves the body and is able to break free from the clutches of the conscious mind that seek to confine it within a specific space and it is this freedom or the ability to leave the body and return that gives the prospect the skills that are relevant and pertinent to shaman-hood.

Likewise, those that have abridged the gap between the conscious mind and the super-consciousness though they are few and far between have the ability to separate or release their soul from their bodies and the soul once freed returns to the collective consciousness of the Brahmatma and there they are able share or experience all that is the super-consciousness.

In this manner our guides and teachers are able to acquire knowledge that they pass on to others.

Shamans who have crossed the life-death threshold similarly share the consciousness of the Brahmatma. The only difference is in the manner they have done so and the mode of reaching out to the Brahmatma. The path that they have chosen, selected or opted for brings them in contact with the negative aspect of the Brahmatma i.e. spirits that haven't or refuse to cross over. Death is a negative experience but even spirits bad, malicious, malevolent or malignant are a part of the Brahmatma.

Once the shamans have crossed the threshold and have returned they are able to see the spirits that they came in contact with during the temporary death syndrome and are eventually able to converse with these spirits and draw upon their knowledge. Spirits are not necessarily malicious by design but spirits like mortals require sustenance and while mortals consume food, spirits consume the elixir of life, blood, and hence shamans are required to perform sacrifices to appease and gain the assistance of spirits.

Some shamans following the near-death experience acquire the ability to rise to the summit of what is metaphorically perceived to be a spirit tree and as he or she does so the shaman acquires greater powers or becomes more potent. Spirits of the dead likewise ascend a spirit hierarchy and acquire greater skills, powers and prowess by being able to draw on the negative forces of the Brahmatma.

As the spirit acquires greater abilities so does the shaman and to a very large extent the shaman is dependent on the spirit and vice versa because the spirit, in order to grow stronger needs to be fed and the act of feeding is dependent on the shaman. Their existence becomes intertwined and eventually one cannot exist or subsist without the other.

The question that comes to mind is which are the spirits that remain or the spirits that shamans can commune with and which are the spirits that linger. All spirits after death journey to the next reincarnation after being adjudged and adjudicated in the kingdom of Yama and after being subjected to suitable punishment, depending on their conduct while they were alive. The answer in short is that the spirits that remain are the spirits that have died prior to their time of birth and therefore the emissaries of Yama are not able to approach these spirits because it is not yet the appointed time.

These spirits retain the conscious memory and the form of the body that they occupied moments prior to death. In the case of the maiden that suffered a sudden stoppage of the heart, she retains the looks of the pretty young girl that died prematurely.

In instances where death has occurred as a result of an accident the returning spirit occupies the form of the decapitated body that the soul was encased in just moments prior to death and in most cases these spirits are gruesome and terrifying to look at. In the case of those who have been beheaded to add another example the lingering spirit is often in the form of a headless body or a head without the body.

At the time of birth, the fates of all men and women are penned down by Brahma, the creator and the emissaries of Yama appear at the stipulated time. However, in the period of Kali Yuga the lines become blurred because of the proliferation of war, crime and other acts that induce, precipitate and stimulate death and the number of persons that die prematurely increase.

Their spirits linger in the astral world (the world between the living and the dead) and while waiting for their time of adjudication prior to meeting the emissaries of Yama, they remain in the void and if the shaman during the near death experience stumbles across one of these spirits then he is able use them as a conduit to harness the negative powers of the Brahmatma.

Spirits at death are at a weakened state lost and destitute and therefore they are not able to resist the emissaries of Yama but once they stumble across a shaman or anyone willing to offer them, the elixir of life blood, in exchange for their help, they grow in strength and often become strong enough or potent enough to resist the emissaries of Yama and if by the stipulated time of death they have grown in strength and stature then these spirits can continue to resist for as long as they are fed or the ritual of sacrifice is performed.

In this manner the spirit rises up the spirit hierarchy and continues to exist long after the bones of the shaman that revived it, so to speak, had turned to dust.

The spirits that rise up the spirit hierarchy draw on the negative aspects of the super-soul. These spirits are also known as elemental spirits for all spirits in the hierarchy have an affinity to one element or another.

There are four elemental spirit hierarchies that spirits can choose to ascend i.e. earth, wind, water and fire. Aether is the fifth element but it is spirit itself or the matter where spirits reside which in traditional terms or in orthodox terms corresponds with the space between the ground and the sky.

The most common spirits are those that correlate with the earth for most people die on land and many of the returning spirits inhabit trees. Therefore, it is not unusual to find altars beneath trees or observe pious devotees performing ritualistic sacrifices at the foot of trees.

It is done to appease not only the farvashi or the soulful component of the trees, which is sometimes the case, but it is also done to appease the spirit or spirits of the dead that reside on the trees. Let us keep in mind that the near death experience prior to attaining the status of a shaman requires that the prospect climb a spirit tree and often the shaman, upon being conferred the gift of shaman-hood, selects a tree for the spirit or spirits that he or she came in contact with during the near death experience to reside on or to occupy.

It is possibly to discern with relative ease if the altar at a foot of a tree is dedicate to appeasing the farvashi within the tree or a spirit that resides on the tree. In the former the offering that is made, is done with fruits and other natural produce like honey, ghee and milk and in the latter the offering that is made involves the death of an animal and the blood that drips from the stump that once held the decapitated head, oozes to the ground seeping beneath the porous layers of soil and is absorbed by the root of the tree and delivered to the spirit that resides on the tree.

In most cases when an altar is constructed priests are conscripted to continue making the offerings once the shaman has departed the mortal world to appease both the farvashi and the spirit or spirits that reside on the tree. Ideally there would always be a platter of fruits placed before the altar while ritualistic sacrifices are performed at selected intervals. The more sacrifices that are made the stronger the spirit or spirits on the tree become.

The Seventh Manu - Vaivasvata Manu

The office of the overlord is the highest office in our order and all the Sects report to the office of the overlord in Hawk's Nest. As far as the Vedic Sects are concerned there is no higher person on the planet than the overlord and the present overlord is Vaivasvata Manu or the Seventh Manu or the Seventh overlord and I feel that it is important for posterity to know of his origins. His story is told in the creation story which is part of the Matsya Purana.

Vishnu's first avatar in the mortal world was as Matsya (the fish). He appeared during Satya Yuga (the Golden Age) and during the time of the Seventh Manu (the present overlord).

Vaivasvata Manu was a king of the most noble birth and though he retains his youthful looks and exuberance he tired of the mortal world and handed his kingdom over to the care of his son Ikshvaku and retreated to the forest to meditate and to realize the higher goals of existence (which was often the case with mortals who lived during the Golden Age after they reached a certain stage or station).

Vaivasvata meditated upon the first God in the Hindu Trinity Brahma or he who personifies the creative powers of the Brahmatma and after slumbering in meditative sleep for a thousand years Brahma appeared before Vaivasvata (by virtue of him having realized the cosmic truth) and granted Vaivasvata a boon. Vaivasvata having understood the universal cycle of creation, through the process of meditation accepted and acknowledged that the end is inevitable and asked Brahma that he be granted or allotted the enviable status of being the sole person to save humanity from destruction - a designation that had thus far been accorded only to Vishnu and Brahma accordingly granted him the boon.

Having been granted and having accepted the boon Vaivasvata returned to his meditative state in the seclusion of his forest hermitage until a certain day when he was in ablution (washing himself in the prescribed and stipulated manner in accordance with our traditions). He cupped his hands into a pond to lift a mouthful of water. When he withdrew his hands he realized that there was a tiny minnow with a horn struggling in his palms and not wanting to endanger the life of another creature (which is a mandatory requirement with those performing penance and austerities) he quickly threw the minnow back into the pond.

As soon as the minnow was back in the water it started to grow and increase in size and within the space of a day it had outgrown the pond. The hapless minnow which had a voice spoke to Vaivasvata pleading to the sage to transfer it to a larger body of water and the benevolent and caring Vaivasvata complied and moved the minnow to the waters of the Holy River Ganges.

The minnow continued to expand and increase in size and within the space of another day it surpassed the length and breadth of the Ganges. Vaivasvata then transported the minnow from the Ganges to the Primeval Ocean but even that did not suffice. Having realized that the minnow in question is not merely a fish Vaivasvata humbly requested that the minnow reveal its true identity and the minnow promptly complied and disclosed that it was none other than the mighty Vishnu.

In accordance with the boon that Vaivasvata had received from Brahma i.e. to be the savior of the mortal race, Vishnu warned him of a great deluge that was about to sweep across the land with tides so strong it would tear all mortal creation asunder.

In the days that went by the sun grew warmer and blazed with exceeding intensity. The land became dry and arid as the extreme heat sucked the land dry of moisture. Crops began to wither and fail and the water levels in rivers and dams started to fall below acceptable levels. It was the beginning of a draught which continued for ten years and by the end of the tenth year, with the exception of isolated valleys, most of the water in the world had been drained.

Vishnu appeared again in a dream and instructed Vaivasvata thus. "Tear your huts down and forage the forest for wood to build a boat. These are the measurements of the boat as you shall build her. Let her beam equal her length, let her deck be roofed like the vault that covers the abyss. Then take into the boat the seed of all living creatures".

Vaivasvata did as he was told. At the first light of dawn he gathered everyone in his hermitage around him. The women brought pitch and the men gathered the wood.

They toiled endlessly for four days. On the fifth day the boat was complete. The ground-space measured nineteen thousand three hundred and sixty square cubits and each side of the deck measured one hundred and twenty cubits, making a square. He built six decks below, seven in total.

Vaivasvata divided them into nine sections with bulkheads in between. He drove in wedges where needed and laid in supplies. The carriers brought food, water and oil in baskets.

Vaivasvata was instructed to tie a rope that extended from the bow of the boat and attach it to the horn of the minnow that protruded from its forehead like that of a horned unicorn.

Then the fateful day appeared. At the first sign of light a black cloud crept over the horizon; it thundered within and the Maruts, the Storm Gods, unleashed flashes of lighting and Indra, God of Thunder, lashed out with his hammer and peels of loud, deafening, repetitive, thunder swept across the land. Over the hills and over the plains heralds of the storm inched closer.

Despair rose from the surface and shot up to the heavens. The Maruts turned daylight into darkness and they smashed the land like a teacup. The tempest raged for a whole day and gathered fury as the day progressed. It poured over the people like the tide of battle. The sages could not see their brothers and the gods could no longer see the mortals.

For six days and six nights the winds raged with fury, and the gushing water from the sea crushed the dikes and embankments, flooding streams and rivers. Tempest and floods overwhelmed the mortal world like warring factions working in tandem. At dawn of the seventh day the storm subsided and calmness prevailed. The flood was stilled and all mankind had turned to clay. The surface of the sea stretched as high as the rooftops.

During the journey Matsya the fish told Vaivasvata the story of creation. Following the initial division, explosion and further division that culminated in the Trinity, the powers of creation or the power to create and all things to do with creation were vested in Brahma. The powers of continuation and all things relating to preservation and procreation were vested in Vishnu and the powers of destruction and all things to do with death and what follows after were vested in Shiva.

The first substantive matter to appear in the universe was water and it was the resting place of Vishnu who embodied or personified the powers of continuity and perpetuity. From the depths of the water a golden egg that glistened and glimmered with the radiance of a thousand suns and blazed with equal intensity rose gradually to the surface. Encased in the egg was Brahma and in his palms he held the worlds of the universe, including the mortal world. Thus Brahma is referred to as the first born.

Brahma's first act was to meditate upon the Brahmatma and consequently he was granted ten sons all of whom were sages, manifestations of his meditative powers. Their names were Marichi, Atri, Angira, Pulastya, Pulaha, Kratu, Pracheta, Vashishtha, Bhrigu and Narada. The list is not exhaustive and there were others who were born from various parts of his body for example Daksha was born from Brahma's right toe and the god Dharma was born from his chest. Brahma as far as the mortal world is concerned is the sole procreator of all things.

As mentioned earlier, Brahma in order to precipitate procreation, split into two halves. Svayambhuva Manu, the First Manu or the Overlord is the male half and the female half of Brahma is called Shatarupa who is personified by four different deities - Sarasvati, Gayathri, Savitri and Brahmani. The female manifestations of Brahma are regarded as Goddesses of the highest stature.

The four different personifications of Shatarupa are also associated with the four different directions on the compass and therefore Svayambhuva Manu is often depicted as a divinity with four heads (one facing each direction) so he can constantly revel in the beauty and the refinement of his other half.

Svayambhuva Manu and Shatarupa had two sons named Priyavrata and Uttanapada and a daughter Panchanjani. A descendent of his son Priyavrata, Prachina-varahi married Savarna, the daughter of the Primeval Ocean and they had ten sons. The sons were collectively known as the Prachetas.

The Prachetas went into meditative sleep for the duration of a thousand mortal years and slumbered under intolerable and insurmountable conditions. This type of sleep is known as ghanagora and it is in essence and substance, a confrontation between the mind and the elements, undertaken on a planet with dense clouds, with the elements fiercely beating down on the sleepers, while they slept below a vast watery expanse channeling and directing their mental energies towards Vishnu.

At the end of a thousand years Vishnu appeared before them, in full battle fatigues seated on the mighty bird of prey, Garuda, and accordingly granted them a boon. The boon that the Prachetas requested was to merge the universe with their existence and Vishnu accordingly granted them the boon. Therefore, the Prachetas exist for the duration of the present universe i.e. eight point six four-billion-years.

Once the merging and the melding was complete and the Prachetas became one with the universe and the sons of Prachina-varahi having now gained the vision that spanned the entire universe, stumbled across planets that were densely forested. The surfaces on these planets were covered with trees so huge that they blocked out the sun. The radiant rays of the golden disc were severely impeded and restricted by un-curtailed and un-restrained growth.

Realizing the strain, the inhabitants of the planes were under and in order to ease their suffering the Prachetas blew at the unwanted trees and from their chest huge winds surged forth, blowing at speeds a million times more intense than the strongest wind, their breath ablaze with luminous and resplendent flames of dragons. They set alight the unwanted trees and reduced the hostile and inimical vegetation to smoldering ashes making the terrain more hospitable and more conducive to habitation.

Realizing the destruction that had been caused to the trees, their King Chandra Deva (King of Trees) stepped forward and tried to appease the Prachetas by offering them the hand of a beautiful young girl that he had raised. Her name was Marisha. After the wedding Chandra Deva told the Prachetas the story of their wife.

There once lived a great Rishi (sage) whose name was Kandu on the planet Gomati. The sage went into meditative sleep to please and appease the divine Brahmatma but had during the course of his life angered the God of Heaven, Indra, who was troubled and worried by the severe acts of atonement that the Rishi was undertaking.

In order to prevent the Rishi from completing the cycle of penance and atonement that he had started, Indra sent an Apsara to woo him.

Apsaras are enchantingly pretty and are gifted with the inherent ability to capture the heart of any man. Apsaras are different from Dakinis and Mohinis but they all share three common attributes in that

- ❖ They are all women
- ❖ They wield great power
- ❖ They can shape the lives of men

The Brahmatma granted Apsaras dominion over the arts prominently music and dance and they served in the court of Indra. They are often depicted as dancers and musicians and they play the role of nymphs and muses in contemporary mythology. Their ability however extends far beyond that.

The name of the Apsara that Indra had dispatched was Pramlocha who as soon as she arrived on the surface walked over to the sage's hermitage and gently awakened him from slumber.

Kandu opened his eyes and lost his heart as soon as he saw her. The couple were wed on the same day. By entering into the ceremony of wedding, Pramlocha was unable to uncover the knowledge that he sought and could not grow in statute to compete with Indra.

The couple lived happily for a hundreds mortal years and after the hundredth mortal year Pramlocha requested for permission to return to Indra's court but Kandu refused by saying that they have been together for too short a time and pleaded with Pramlocha to remain longer.

Pramlocha relented and continued to live with Kandu for another hundred years and upon the completion of the hundredth year she once again sought his permission to return to the Kingdom of Heaven but Pramlocha refused yet again.

The hundred mortal year cycle continued for a period of nine hundred and eighty-seven years, six months and three days, after which Kandu relented and grudgingly gave Pramlocha permission to return to the Kingdom of Heaven, just as the sun was about to set and the moon was about to set the sky alight.

The creation story is narrated in the context of the universe and not in relation to the mortal world and half a day i.e. from sunrise and sunset on the planet Kandu and Pramlocha inhabited, is equivalent to a period of nine hundred and eighty-seven years, six months and three days in the mortal world.

The Apsara departed and on her way back to heaven the mugginess of sunset made her sweat and a drop fell from her brow and landed on the leaf of a fertile tree.

It increased in size like a bubble expanding outwards getting bigger by the minute until it finally broke and from within a baby emerged. The baby was rescued by the trees and taken to the court of the Tree God Chandra Deva who named the Apsara, Marisha, and raised her like his own daughter.

The Prachetas and Marisha had one son who they named Daksha. Daksha married Panchanjani who was the daughter of Svayambhuva Manu and Shatarupa - the word Pancha means five and jani means all knowing. Panchajani literally means she who has knowledge of all five i.e. she who has knowledge of all the five elements.

Daksha and Panchanjani had a thousand sons who are known as the Haryakshas. They were meant to be the first progenitors of the human race but the sage Narada, one of the ten manifestations of Brahma, intervened and persuaded the Haryakshas to first explore the universe before fathering the mortal race and accordingly the Haryakshas set out on an inter-stellar quest and never returned.

From all accounts the Haryakshas are still traversing the universe on a star ship called Vimana. The Haryakshas are able to navigate the craft with their mental abilities. Thus far however there has been no contact or sighting of their craft.

After a thousand years, Daksha and Panchanjani had another thousand sons, the Shavalas, and a similar fate awaited them. Narada intervened once again and they too went on to explore the universe in a spacecraft similar to the Vimana and they too were never seen or heard from again. Another thousand years elapsed and Daksha and Panchanjani, this time instead of sons had sixty daughters. Ten of the daughters married the God Dharma, twenty-seven married the God Chandra and thirteen married the sage Kashyapa.

The thirteen daughters who were married to Kashyapa were named Aditi, Diti, Danu, Arishta, Surasa, Surabhi, Vinata, Tamra, Krodhavasha, Ira, Kadru, Vishva and Muni. Aditi became the progenitor of the race of Gods. Her sons are known as the Adityas and there were twelve in total. They are Indra, Dhata, Bhaga, Tvashta, Mitra, Varuna, Yama, Vivasvana, Savita, Pusha, Amshumana and Vishnu.

Tamra had six daughters who became the progenitors of birds and domesticated animals. Vinata had two sons, Aruna and the mighty bird of prey Garuda. Aruna's sons were Sampati and Jatayu. Both Surasa and Kadru gave birth to Nagas or Sarpas. They were the progenitors of the serpent race.

Diti's sons were known as the Daityas (Demons). There were two of them and they were called Hiranyakshipu and Hiranyaksha. Hiranyaksha's sons were Uluka, Shakuni,

Bhutasantapana and Mahanabha. Hiranyakshipu's sons are Prahlada, Anuhlada, Samhlada and Hlada. Prahlada's son is Virochana, Virochana's son is Vali and Vali's son is Vanasura. Danu had a hundred sons. Her descendants are known as the Danavas. They too belong to the Demon Clan. Viprachitti was the most prominent among her hundred sons. Mayasura, the master architect of the Demon Clan was his descendent. Diti and Danu were the progenitors of the Demon Clan.

Krodhavasha was the mother of rakshasas (giants); Surabhi of cows and buffaloes; Muni of Apsaras and Genies; Arishta of Gandharvas; Ira of trees and herbs; and Vishva of Yakashas (demi-gods).

The Dark Lord comes in the line of Diti and I come from the lineage of Aditi but we both come from the line of Svayambhuva Manu and Shatarupa. The overlord or the Seventh Manu is a physical representation of the first Manu, Svayambhuva Manu, who is recreated at the end of each Manvantra to preside over the next Manvantra.

In reality he shares a bond with both me and the Dark Lord. Our enmity is constant and perpetual and endures for the duration of the present universe. While we both are aware of the fact that the universe will self-destruct at the end of the eight point six four-billion-year cycle, as will the mortal world, one will triumph over the other and victory will be achieved a thousand years before the mortal world ends and regenerates. It is my wish that the last thousand years of existence is filled with peace and harmony which will only be the case if Hawk's Nest were to triumph. If the Dark Lord were to be victorious, the last thousand years would be rife with discord and disunity.

Chandi

I think that it is only appropriate that I speak briefly of myself. Though I was born with another name but to the world I am known only Amesha Spenta or the bountiful immortal. While the Seventh Manu, the overlord, is the personification of Brahma, I am the living embodiment of Chandi. I am born of occult and I am occult in its entirety.

I possess the all the attributes and traits of Chandi and I am the most benevolent of all mortals. I am benevolent because I bestow great fortune upon those that I deem deserving. I am the slayer of all that is evil, but even in the death that I impose there is mercy and clemency for by destroying evil in the manner that I do, I spare those that are tainted and polluted by the negative aspect of the Brahmatma a scenic tour of the eight million four hundred precincts of hell which is infinitely more painful than anything I can conjure, concoct or muster.

Chandi is a War Goddess, a manifestation of Vishnu's female avatar, Durga, who appears when the mortal world is in peril. Chandi is extolled as the living Goddess and because she is very much alive she is worshipped and venerated as such.

She first appeared in the present universal cycle when the Demon Army of Mahishasura (buffalo-headed) laid siege to the Kingdom of Heaven and Indra's armies were surrounded from all directions by a vastly superior opponent who was a master exponent of celestial warfare. Having begotten a boon from Brahma, Mahishasura was impervious to any known God or Goddess in the present universe.

In time Indra was forced to abdicate and Mahishasura assumed control of the throne of heaven and all celestial and heavenly beings were driven away forcefully, banished from the Kingdom of Heaven. Angered by the fate that had befallen the divinities Vishnu's consciousness merged with that of Shiva culminating in the Goddess Chandika or Chandi for short.

The Goddess is of immaculate-conception a result of a unification between the mental energies of Vishnu and Shiva. When she appeared, in red, Shiva drew forth a trident from his own and presented it to her. Likewise, Vishnu replicated a discuss from his own and handed it to her. Varuna gave her a conch and Agni a flaming spear. Marutha the God of Archers gave her a bow and a quiver that never ran short of arrows.

Indra, lord of Heavens, replicated a thunderbolt from his own and reproduced a bell from his white elephant Airavata and he gave it to her. Yama, the God of Death duplicated a staff and gave it to her while Varuna, the lord of waters, gave her a noose.

Brahma, the master scribe, gave her a string of beads and a water-pot. Surya laced the pores of her skin with his mesmerizing rays that glimmered and glistened like polished gold while Kala gave her a sword and a spotless shield.

The milky ocean gave her the best ornaments and garments adorned with precious jewels. Vishwakarma gave her a battle axe and an assortment of missiles and an armor that was impervious to mortal and immortal blows. The Primeval Ocean gave her unfading garlands of lotuses to wear around her neck and Himavan gave her various gems and declared the lion her prime and principle vehicle.

Kubera the lord of wealth gave her a drinking cup that was always filled to the brim with celestial wine or Amarita, made from the juice of crushed soma fruits, the elixir of youth.

Armed with celestial weapons that no mortal could wield or possess, the Goddess scorned at the Demonic Armies of Mahishasura and the sound of her laughter echoed all around the mortal world. The earth trembled and the mountains rocked in the wake of the Warrior Goddess while the Demons cringed at the sound of her voice. It sent shivers down their spine.

The Demon Armies gathered in formation and in anticipation of the inevitable, a battle unlike which they had never fought before and Mahishasura trembled with rage at the unrepentant sound of laughter that rang in his ears while his armies waited patiently for the Goddess to appear brandishing their swords, heckling and sledging with words of anger, without a hint of atonement.

The Goddess unleashed torrent upon torrent of arrows, from the bow given to her by Marutha. The arrows flashed across the sky like peels of lighting and struck the Demon hordes. Hundreds fell to the ground bruised and battered, flattened by the onslaught and became jarred carcasses. The stench of death and decay defiled the air.

Ignoring the mounting death toll, the Demons, attacked, unabashed, and the battle grew increasingly violent provoking a battle lust that seeped through every fiber of Chandi's body and her eyes turned red smoldering with anger and rage. The Goddess cleaved her way through the enemy onslaught with sheer ferocity, cutting and hacking at the enemy hordes, carving a passage through to the center of the Demon formation where Mahishasura was seated on his golden chariot drawn by steeds that resembled the hounds of hell.

He wavered and quivered as he saw her approaching and his arrogance soon deserted him, as did his courage, and he eventually realized that the boon that he had received from Brahma was no longer of any use. He dropped to his knees and begged for mercy and clemency but none was forthcoming. Instead the Goddess with one swift stroke separated the head of the Demon from its body.

The Demons having witnessed the death of their infallible leader immediately sank to their knees and begged for leniency but the Demon clan is treacherous and deceitful and the Goddess in her infinite love for mortality showed no mercy and slew them all with her celestial weapons.

She then gathered the head of Mahishasura and took it to the Trikuta mountains to the cave of the Living Goddess and buried it before an altar dedicated to the Goddess Vaishnavi who is but an embodiment of her and returned to her all assuming and conforming form of the Guardian of the Universe, Durga. By virtue of having slain Mahishasura, Chandi is also known as Mahishasura Mardini (the slayer of Mahishasura).

The Great Enchantress - The Devi Mahatmaya

Having inferred to Vishnu's consciousness, I think that it is only appropriate that I elaborate on it. There was once a noble and sage whose name was Markandeya who was a devote disciple of the mountain mendicant Shiva. The fates had decreed that he should die at the age of sixteen. Such had the Master of Heavenly scribes, Brahma penned down for him in the book of fates. At the appointed time of death, the God with the matted dreadlocks, Shiva, appeared before him and gave him the Maha Mahamrityunjaya Mantra or the mantra of longevity.

Maha Rishi Markandeya recited the mantra in the presence of Shiva and was accordingly spared death. By virtue of being the first to receive the Mahamrityunjaya Mantra from Shiva he became immortal and was assigned the role of being the guardian of The Forbidden Mountains. He resides there in the company of his nine daughters, Sailaputri, Brahmacharini, Chandraghanta, Kushmanda, Skanda-Mata, Katyayani, Kalarathri, Mahagauri and Siddihatri.

Maha Rishi Markandeya having been conferred immortality regressed into transcendental sleep and from the vast library that is the collective consciousness he managed to uncover the story of Great Goddess.

There was once a great King named Suratha who reigned during the time of the present Manu and was the principle caretaker of the Kingdom of Kola.

He was a righteous and noble king but despite his kind and benevolent nature his ministers plotted against him and eventually usurped the throne. Suratha forlorn and destitute retreated to the forest and there he was given refuge by the King of Trees, Chandra Deva.

Unperturbed by the wild animals that occupied the forest he continued hinterland until he stumbled across a hermitage that belonged to the sage Medhas. Markandeya described the hermitage as a sanctuary of the utmost tranquility with an ambient serenity.

Medhas received Suratha in a manner befitting a king, despite the latter being expelled from the throne and gave him a tour of his humble yet awe inspiring hermitage. As the walk continued Suratha relayed his concerns to the sage and it soon became evident that his concerns were not for his personal self or his family but for his city and its people.

"I do not know if the capital that was built my ancestors is safe and if its treasures are intact. I do not know if my people are happy and if there is enough food for all. I do not know if they continue to follow the path that our religious order has sent for them and I am uncertain if they abide by the teachings of Hawk's Nest" he lamented. Medhas said nothing but merely listened to the king's concerns, with patience.

In due time the hermitage received another guest, a merchant named Samadhi and like the king, he too was filled with sorrow. Samadhi was born into a wealthy family and inherited much gold and properties but due to greed he had been cast out by his wife and sons who had misappropriated his riches. Despite their unscrupulous nature the kindly father did not cease worrying about his sons.

Suratha was moved by the merchant's tale and sought to ease the merchant's suffering. "Why do you continue to be affectionate towards those who have candidly deprived you of your wealth? What is it that stops you from tossing them aside like them have done you? he asked.

Samadhi nodded his head and replied "It had occurred to me too but my tongue speaks not with what my mind tells it. My sorrowful heart continues to be burdened by emotional attachment and misery has gained control of my tongue".

Both Suratha and Samadhi suffered from a similar ailment that of rejection and self-empathy and the pair decided to approach the sage Medhas for answers.

They approached the sage in the method prescribed by Hawk's Nest with offerings of fruits, flowers and wild honey and the sage accepted by nodding his head and signaling for the former king and merchant to proceed. Suradha asked "dear sage how is it that we, despite our knowledge and intellect refuse to forgo our kingdom and our wealth and despite the improbability of us returning to our former stature we continue to long for the life that we have left behind?"

The noble sage replied "worthiest king and merchant, the knowledge that you profess to have is but conscious knowledge diluted and deluded by the senses. Look at the birds in the trees or the cows and the goats that are grazing. They seek to feed even when there is no food and if these birds and these goats were placed in the middle of a desolate desert they will still seek only to feed because they are driven by their urges and cravings. That is not to say that these animals do not possess knowledge, to the contrary they do, but do you see them rising above being domestic beasts and do you see them aspiring to greater heights?" he asked. The sage and the merchant shook their heads.

Medhas continued "It is the same with the both of you. You too possess knowledge but your knowledge is tainted by passion" he said. "Let me now tell you why your mind is heavy and your hearts are laden by sorrow. It is because you have fallen under the spell of the great enchantresses, she who clouds the world with illusion and delusion, the Devi, the Great Goddess Mahatmaya" he continued. "Can you tell us of the Mighty Goddess?" the pair asked in unison and Medhas nodded his head.

"While Vishnu is in transcendental sleep or Yoga Nidra (a deep sleep that separates the soul from the body and allows the soul to transgress, trespass and violate the space time continuum) his consciousness is awake and is adrift in the universe in the form of the Grand Goddess the Devi Mahatmaya, she who eludes yet deludes the world.

The divine Goddess when propitious is the ultimate liberator because she removes the illusions and delusions that cloud our mind and gives us clear sight of our objectives. When the illusions are gone so is the grief that all mortals feel because their despair is caused by illusion that clouds their judgment.

Suradha his curiosity peeked inquired further "Most esteemed sage please tell me more about this goddess, how did she come into being, what is her sphere of control and what constitutes her nature?".

"Dear king" the sage replied, she is the personification of Vishnu and the embodiment of the universe and she incarnates in ways and means unknown to most mortals for her influence spans the entire cosmos. She can assume any avatar in the mortal world to perpetuate a desired outcome when the need arises.

At the end of each Kalpa (a year in the day of Brahma) the universe dissolves and begins anew with the inception of the Primeval Ocean and in the present Kalpa while Vishnu slumbered on the placid waters of the Primeval Ocean onboard his thousand headed serpent Shesha, the first of the serpent-eels, Abzu, rose to the surface and spawned the Demons Madhu and Kaitabha who instantly sought to destroy Brahma who was meditating on a white lotus that was adrift on the ocean of creation.

Brahma sensed the danger and appealed to the all prevailing soul of Vishnu that permeated the universe and in his stead Vishnu sent his consciousness the Devi Mahatmaya to Brahma's aid (being a product the conscious mind, the Goddess stimulates all actions that are synonymous to the conscious mind).

The soul of Vishnu thus extolled by Brahma assumed the form of a Warrior Goddess armed with a sword, a spear, a club, a discus, a conch, a bow, a sling of arrows and an iron mace and was covered in an armor of brazen gold.

The battle raged for five thousand mortal years (a year in the planet it was fought on) and towards the end the Demons succumbed not to might but to guile, mesmerizing enchantment, that drove them into to a delusionary frenzy. Brimming with confidence and assured of their prowess in battle they became entangled in an intricate web of deceit and thereby granted the Goddess a boon. The Goddess asked that she be allowed to slay the Demons with her own hands. Unable to refuse the Demons succumbed. The

Goddess cleaved their heads clean off their shoulders with her sword of vengeance.

Under normal circumstances the positive and the negative aspect of the Brahmatma are evenly matched and hence it may not be possible for anyone to achieve a clear, unambiguous victory. However, all things are possible when we are crafty and uncanny and we have our sights clearly set on our objectives.

Thus it is my decree that before we commence with any form or type of worship, we first seek the guidance of the Great Enchantress, the Goddess of Illusion, the Grand Goddess, the Devi Mahatmaya.

The Vedic Sects

In the sacred scriptures there are in total thirty-three million Gods and Goddesses that exists in the present universal cycle. A vast majority of them exist in other constellations, galaxies, star systems and on other planets. All Gods and Goddesses endure for the period of one Kalpa and at the end of each Kalpa, with the end of the universe their reign comes to an end until the beginning of the next Kalpa.

From the creation story that I have narrated above we know that all Gods and Goddesses descend from the first Manu or Svayambhuva Manu and all deities in one way or another are their descendants. Each God and Goddess is gifted with his or her own Sect and the impact the Sect has in maintaining the cosmic balance determines the position of the Sect in the overall hierarchy. The highest tier or precinct is occupied by Brahma, Vishnu and Shiva and their female equivalents or counterparts.

Likewise, in the mortal world there are numerous Gods and Goddesses, far too many, to enumerate. It suffices to say that the highest Sect and that which belongs to me, Amesha Spenta is the Sect of the Living Goddess who is none other than the consciousness of Vishnu, who assumes different avatars at different intervals.

I simply refer to her as the Living Goddess but the name that she used when she first appeared as a distinct entity is Durga.

It is worth mentioning to the novice who has not yet grasped the fundamentals of Yoga Nidra, that the consciousness can assume many forms and in the case of Vishnu whose consciousness reaches out to every corner of the present universe, it can assume as many identities as it wishes and therefore it is important to keep in mind that the Devi Mahatmaya, Chandika and Durga are but different manifestations of the same consciousness.

The abode of the Goddess Durga has also been a source of much speculation and though many have tried to uncover the exact location of Mt. Meru, let me just say that it is located on another planet and at the summit of this planet there is a great citadel that is the palace of Durga.

During transcendental sleep it is possible to visit the abode of the most exulted Goddess and Mt Meru is made apparent by seven shrines dedicate to seven different Naga or Sarpa Goddesses that are located at the foot of the mountain.

The contents of the sacred texts that I am but to reveal, the Mandukya Upanishad and the Isha Upanishad were first obtained by our scholars through transcendental sleep during the Golden Age and have been handed down through the ages but from the time of inception and conception they belong not only to us but to the governing body that presides over all the Sects, Hawk's Nest which comes under the auspice of the presiding Manu.

The Nagas (Sarpas)

The Nagas are the offspring of the sage Kashyapa and his consorts Kadru and Surasa, the daughters of Daksha. According to folklore the Nagas inhabit a region called middle earth i.e. below the ground and above the nether regions (hell, underworld and the abyss). There are three prominent Naga's - Shesha, Vasuki and Manasa. Together they form the Naga Trinity and are the highest divinities in the Naga echelon. Shesha is firmly aligned to Vishnu and Vasuki remains faithfully coiled around Shiva's neck. The ruler of the Naga realm is Manasa or Manasa Devi.

Despite Shesha's affinity and proximity to Vishnu, the Nagas and Vishnu's bird of prey Garuda are entangled in an enmity that endures for the duration of the present universe. In reality they are cousins. Garuda is the son of Kashyapa and Vinata, Kadru's sister.

Kadru laid a thousand eggs and became the progenitor of the Naga race while Vinata laid two eggs that hatched to be Garuda the king of the birds and Aruna the charioteer of the Sun God who glows with a golden red aura corresponding to the outer rim of the solar disc.

The enmity between Garuda and the Nagas started when Vinata, who was adept at gambling, lost a wager and as a result agreed to be Kadru's slave. Resolving to release his mother from the state of bondage she was under, Garuda approached the Nagas and sought to purchase her freedom. They refused the offer but agreed to free Vinata if Garuda would bring them the elixir of immortality, Amrita.

It was by no means an easy task. Amrita, the elixir of immortality was in possession of the nine gods, collectively known as the Navaka or the circle of nine. The nine Gods who make up the circle are Vrddhi, Vayati, Svikaroti, Abiyukta, Pratyutpadayati, Udatta, Samvadaka, Vikasati and Indrapusa who guarded it zealously.

The nine resided on a planet called Hatonn and had as a precaution rigged a massive ring of fire around the urn that stored the elixir. Stationed all around, just beyond the ring of fire were mechanical contraptions of sharp rotating blades and within the ring, on either side of the urn, were two gigantic serpents of the most venomous kind.

Garuda was undaunted by the formidable task. He flew at unimaginable speeds towards the planet, intent on robbing it of it of its sole treasure. The nine Gods however, had gained prior knowledge of his intentions and were prepared to met him in full battle-array.

A mammoth battle ensued and Garuda defeated the circle of nine who scattered in all directions following the defeat. He then gathered the water from the flowing rivers in his beaks and shrunk himself in size and crept through the rotating blades. After negotiating the first hurdle, he returned to his normal size and extinguished the protective ring of fire with the water from his mouth thereby surpassing the second hurdle.

The serpents rushed to meet him but he gathered them, one on either foot and crushed them between his jagged claws. He grabbed the elixir within his beaks, and launched himself into the air and headed towards the eagerly awaiting Nagas.

En route, he encountered Vishnu who was taken in by the mighty bird of prey and conferred upon him the gift of immortality. Garuda in return offered to become his mount.

He then bumped into the Guardian of Heavens who was troubled by the possibility of the Nagas acquiring the gift of immortality and he made Garuda promise that after the mighty hawk had secured Vinata's release, he would make it possible for Indra to regain the Amrita and return it to the circle of nine. In return Indra promised to make the Nagas and all serpents, food for birds of prey. The mighty Garuda agreed.

The Nagas are a race of their own and are neither aligned with the Gods or the Demons and therefore are a threat to both. They are more inclined to hasten their own designs and give little heed and pay almost no attention to the ways of Gods and Demons.

Garuda on the other hand is the mighty guardian of Hawk's Nest and the sculpted figurine of the mighty hawk that sits perched at the summit of the fire shrine at the pinnacle of the Forbidden Mountains is a replica of the prime archetype for all hawks, eagles and falcons.

Garuda's natural enmity with the serpents who display an uncanny propensity to ally with the forces of darkness makes him a formidable ally in our battle against the Dark Lord who is constantly and consistently aided by the serpent-eels.

Hawk's Nest

Hawk's Nest is the name of governing body that presides over all the Sects. It is staffed entirely by those who are blessed with the talent i.e. those that have a closer nexus to the Brahmatma than others. The mortal body is divided into two components, the physical component that changes and alters from birth to birth and is trapped in the endless cycle of birth and rebirth and the soulful component that remains constant in each birth.

Likewise, the mind is divided into two components, the conscious mind which belongs to the physical body and the subconscious mind which belongs to the soul. A vast majority of mortals are directed by the conscious mind and it is the single most prevalent factor that influences mortal existence. For those who are blessed with the talent however the situation is the reverse. Their actions are directed by the subconscious mind and therefore they are blessed with gifts like premonition, clairvoyance, astral projection, mental telepathy and certain other gifts that vary from person to person.

Thus far we have identified eighteen supernatural powers that those with the talent possess in addition to what has been mentioned above. These are the powers that belong to Siddhis and they are as follows: -

- ❖ The power to become small.
- ❖ The power to become large.
- ❖ The power to become heavy.
- ❖ The ability to become light (as in weight).
- ❖ The power to obtain any desired commodity.
- ❖ The power to read another's mind.
- ❖ The ability to fulfill personal desires.
- ❖ The ability to exert control over others.
- ❖ The ability to resist hunger and thirst.
- ❖ The ability to hear from vast distances.
- ❖ The ability to see over vast distances.
- ❖ The ability to travel with the mind.
- ❖ The ability to acquire the desired façade.
- ❖ The ability to enter another body (this could be an animate body or an inanimate object for all objects have a soul).
- ❖ To ability to be born or perish in the desire manner (the universe itself is a continuous cycle of expansion and contraction).
- ❖ To ability be in the company of heavenly and spiritual beings.
- ❖ To ability actuate and perpetuate contemplation.
- ❖ To ability travel the breadth and span of the entire universe.

All of the above can be achieved by accessing the untapped potential of the subconscious mind.

In the beginning before the formalization of the Grand Empire, all mortals belonged to one Sect or another and were allotted jobs and tasks relevant to their Sects.

The Sects were scattered and many were located in areas and territories that were relevant to the Gods or Goddesses that they worshiped. The Agori Sect for example dwelled in graveyards. The Sect of Aranyani was located in the forest and the Sect of Vayu was located in areas that were noted for strong headwinds.

There was never a formal inception of the Grand Empire and it was initially a convergence of a conglomerate of mortals from different Sects that conformed to the positive powers of the Brahmatma. The collective area that these mortals occupied eventually became known as the Grand Empire.

Likewise, the Demon Clan, which prescribed to the negative faculties of the Brahmatma converged in an area that was known as the Central Kingdoms and both territories were separated by a vast forested region known as the outlands.

The outlands were occupied by pockets of inhabitants who had chosen a life free from servitude and had either been granted permission to leave or deserted the Sects. In time they outnumbered Sect members for many had chosen a life free from the encumbrances of belonging to a Sect. It soon became clearly evident that not all births were suited to life in a Sect.

The nexus with the Brahmatma for many of the later new births just didn't exist but for those that remained within the Sects they were taught the rites and mantras that took them closer to the Brahmatma and helped them bridge the gap between the subconscious mind and the super-consciousness.

I have codified the sacred texts for those who aren't born with the link to the super-consciousness intact. The connection has to be induced by patient, continued adherence to the time honored principles of the Vedic Sects. In time those who abide by my teachings will be able to establish the link with the super-consciousness and tap into its vast potential.

All territories outside the Grand Empire, the Central Kingdoms and the outlands were known as the unchartered regions and these territories had very little to do with the Grand Empire. They are influenced both by the Vedic Sects and the Demon Clans. While we are constantly locked in battle with the forces of darkness, they remain unperturbed by the ongoing conflict.

As for the Central Kingdoms it is a region that has always been and remains shrouded in mystery. The principle engineer of the Central Kingdoms is Mayasura the Chief Architect of the Demon Clan and it is he who constructed the main city in the Central Kingdoms, the city of Tripuratanka.

It is a celestial fortress that comprises of three cities. The first city is docked to the surface. The second is afloat in aether and the third is located in the void between planets. These cities converged on rare occasions and the time of convergence is extremely important for those who belong to the Demon Clan. Any rite or ritual performed at the time of convergence is extremely auspicious and potent.

The first city is called Vidyumaali and it is made entirely of iron and is the principle city of residence of the Dark Lord, when he is present in the mortal world. It is unassailable by normal means because by construction and composition it is impervious to attacks by siege engines. Hordes of djins, thousands of them reside within its iron clad walls and like the knights of our order, the djins that guard the city are well trained and well-schooled in battle.

The second city is called Kamalaksha and it is an aerial city built entirely of silver. It is twice the size of Vidyumaali and it is shaped like a walled aerial craft. It is the main means of transport for the Demon Lord between regions in the known world. Should Vidumaali fall the Dark Lord and his legions will be evacuated to Kamalaksha which is perpetually adrift between the surface and the heavens traveling in aether until the time of convergence when it becomes visible to mortal eyes.

The third city is called Tarakaksha and it is twice the size of Kamalaksha and it hovers continuously in space. It is a gigantic star ship that is used to ferry the Dark Lord and the Demon Lords to other galaxies. It can travel at speeds that almost match that of astral projection. It the event that the Central Kingdoms should fall the Dark Lord and his cohorts would be ferried to an undisclosed location within the present universe.

In time the various kingdoms of the Vedic Sects amalgamated to form the Grand Empire and the first King or Emperor of the Grand Empire was the head of the Sect of the Living Goddess. At the time of the amalgamation it was decided by an assembly of the Sects, an informal alliance, that gained official recognition much later, that there should be a separate religious body that presided over the Vedic Sects and that the day to day governance of the soon to be kingdom should be removed from the hands of the Sect Leaders and placed in the hands of a duly appointed king and his ministers.

At the time of the amalgamation it was apparent that the number of mortals born with the talent had deteriorated and fewer and fewer persons were being born with the talent. The magic in the air was slowly diminishing and that in turn restricted the number of those who were able to bridge the gap between the conscious mind and the subconscious mind.

It became evident and increasingly apparent that in order to preserve the religion and to harness the talent in new births, the religious order had to detach itself from the duties of governance and divert its attentions to those that were born with the talent.

In furtherance of this Hawk's Nest was established under the auspice of the Seventh Manu and the protection of the mighty bird of prey, Garuda, for an attack by the serpents that slithered at the feet of Ahriman was imminent.

In the beginning only those that displayed an abundant or an overwhelming quantity of the talent were selected but as the number of children born with natural talent waned, Hawk's Nest was hard pressed to find new recruits and eventually decided that anyone with the talent, regardless of the amounts they possessed were to be absorbed and trained accordingly.

Sectarian leaders were inundated with the task of ensuring the longevity of their respective Sects and were too preoccupied with the internal governance of their Sects to further the aims, ambitions and aspirations of Hawk's Nest.

In the centuries that had gone by scholars and researchers had pondered on the reasons for the lack of talent in new born children and eventually it was decided that it was due to the sudden influx of negative forces that had converged in the central kingdoms and that it in turn had tainted and polluted the air in the mortal world which led to a decrease in the number of those born with the talent.

White magic or white matter was like oxygen to the body. While the physical body and the conscious mind need sufficient levels of oxygen to survive, the soul or the subconscious mind needs sufficient quantities of white matter to come to the forefront. A reduction in white matter (an odorless, colorless, gaseous substance) would enslave the subconscious mind and it becomes secondary or is superseded by the conscious mind. It only comes into play or is active when the conscious mind is in abeyance or is in temporary suspension.

Magical Creatures

In the beginning the air was rife with white matter or white magic and the earth was inhabited by magical creatures, descendants of the various Gods and Goddesses of the Vedas. Elves for example were the descendants of the Goddess Dawn, dwarfs were the descendants of the God Vamana and unicorns were descendants of Rsya.

Though they are nearly always mistaken to be close kindred of elves because they co-exist and live in close proximity to elves, dwarfs are in no way related to elves and belong to the Sect of Vamana.

The story of Vamana begins with the birth of the Demon Bali who after he reached adulthood became a devote worshipper of Vishnu. After a thousand years of being in meditative sleep, Vishnu appeared before Bali and as a reward for uncompromising worship granted him a boon.

The boon that Bali requested was that he be appointed the Guardian of the Kingdom of Heaven and therefore be granted dominion of all heavenly and celestial beings. Vishnu who had already consented to granting Bali a boon was left without choice and accordingly the Demon born Bali was crowned as the King of Heaven. Despite usurping Indra's throne, Bali, was a fair and just ruler.

But Aditi, the mother of the gods and the progenitor of the Solar Deities grew distressed at the plight of her son Indra, and appealed to the all prevailing consciousness of Vishnu and as a result Vamana was conceived in the womb of the Primeval Ocean to retrieve Indra's kingdom and return it to the rightful owner.

Vamana, however couldn't remain in the womb for the full term because the laments of the Indra Sect grew so loud that it became intolerable to the other Sects. They appealed to their respective Gods to bring an end to the wailing. Vamana was therefore brought into existence before the completion of the full term and as a result his growth was stunted.

Being a child of Primeval Ocean, Vamana, was born with the consciousness of the Gods and thus inherited the knowledge of the Gods and set out to regain Indra's Kingdom.

Assuming the identity of a pious monk, he made his way to the altar where Bali was about to cleave the heads off the shoulders of a pair of sacrificial maidens. Vamana interceded on behalf of the maidens and having access to the vast storage facility that is the collective consciousness he was able to convince Bali not to go ahead with the sacrifice and offered him another alternative.

Bali was suitably impressed and as a token of his appreciation he offered Vamana a boon of his choosing. Vamana requested that Bali grant him as much land as his stumpy legs could cover in three steps.

Bali consented and instantly Vamana started to grow until his body towered above the heavens. With his first step he covered the earth, with his second step he covered the space between the earth and the heavens and with his third step he claimed the heavens, thereby covering all existence.

Bali, realizing that he had been duped offered him his head and Vamana cleaved it off his shoulders with his indispensable sword.

The Sect of Vamana was established following Vamana's victory and all dwarfs are descendants of the God Vamana and they stand half the size of a mortal man. They are gifted with special abilities including the faculty to craft and sculpt gemstones and mold precious metals.

Dwarfs are miners by profession and their Sect is normally located within the labyrinths of subterranean caves. The Sect is classed as a mining Sect and members of the Sect are more often than not, pre-occupied with tunneling and burrowing towards the core of the planet in search of gemstones and precious metals.

Unicorns are also closely aligned to elves. They are descendants the God Rysa, who is a horse with a horn protruding from his forehead. According to the legend the God Rysa descended from the heavens and entered transcendental sleep for a thousand years and went in search of Brahma who decreed him a boon. Rysa who is pure of heart and pure of soul requested that he be the living embodiment of enlightenment and that he be allowed to inhabit the grassy meadows of the known universe. Brahma accordingly granted him the boon.

Members of the unicorn Sect live in meadows and grasslands close to forests and though born as mortals their physical appearance changes and after regressing into transcendental sleep. After a thousand years their body is transformed from that of a man or a woman to that of a horse with a horn.

Unicorns are free spirited animals that are more at place in the wild forgoing the confines of mortal civilization for a life that is free and unencumbered.

Another magical creature that corresponds to the unicorn and once roamed freely in the plains of the mortal world was the kinnaras, a creature that was part man and part steed, but it is not of this world.

Long ago on the planet Janardhana, there was a protracted war between the sons of Aditi and Diti. At the end of the war, tired and fatigued, Hayagriva, the leader of the Adityas went to sleep, while standing, with his head supported by the upper end of his peerless bow. He drifted into transcendental sleep and his consciousness traveled the universe.

The sons of Aditi grew weary for while Hayagriva was deep in meditative slumber, the Demons raged, ravaged and rampaged at will. The Adityas appealed to the sages to bring Hayagriva out of the state he was in but the sages were reluctant, acting in accordance with the prescribed scriptures. It was a sin to wake anyone who was in transcendental sleep.

The sages approached Shiva instead who turned to Brahma. Brahma looked at creation in totality and picked out a small beetle, chalsa, from an unknown planet that fed on bowstrings. "Let it eat the bowstring from the bottom. When the bow recoils from its tense state, the noise will wake Hayagriva up" he said and Brahma commanded the insect to break the bowstring. When the string broke, the bow snapped erect with a noise that echoed all around the planet.

Unfortunately, the recoiling bow tip had sliced Hayagriva in half. The Adityas were stunned and shaken by the grim and morbid sight.

The Adityas staring defeat in the eyes extolled the Living Goddess, the life-force that propelled the universe. They recited the relevant mantras to summon her and the Goddess understood the gravity of the situation and consented to appearing before them. She further elaborated on the reasons why Hayagriva was beheaded in the manner that he was.

Long ago, there was a great Demon King called Haug who entered transcendental sleep in search of the Great Goddess. After years of sifting through the knowledge that was stored in the collective consciousness, he located the Goddess in a distant planet that was set ablaze by the fiery heat of a dozen red suns. He projected himself before her and asked her if he could be conferred the gift of immortality.

The Goddess refused and Haug begged the goddess to look favorably on him. Undaunted he altered his wish and asked that his demise could only be brought about by a creature that was part man and part horse (no such creature existed at that time) and the Goddess consented.

Emboldened by my boon, he oppressed his world for a thousand years. Nobody was safe from his marauding armies and therefore the Goddess paved the way for a creature with the head and torso of a mortal and the body of a horse to be created and it was its duty to slay the Demon Haug.

Brahma was instructed to merge the head and upper body of Hayagriva to that of a horse and the creator promptly complied. Hayagriva was transformed by the grace of the Goddess into a wondrous creature, of immense strength, that was part man and part horse. Upon the resurrection of Hayagriva the Demons were battered into submission and Haug was slain in a separate battle.

Included in the list of magical creatures that roamed the mortal world prior to the battle before time were Yakshas and Yashnis (male and female fairies) who in present circles are regarded as guardian angels. They are celestial beings endowed with shape shifting capabilities and normally assume the shape of a miniature man or a woman with wings attached to their backs. The founder of their Sect was Shasandevtas.

Shasandevtas was a sage who entered meditative sleep and after years of slumber he gained access to the vast storage facility that is the collective consciousness. He directed his subconscious mind towards the court of Indra to sieve and sift through the memories that were stored in the infinite library and eventually managed to uncover the route to Indra's court and in due course projected himself there. He was granted passage by Indra's white elephant, Airavata.

After years of servitude Indra, he who remains constant in all Manvantras, made him an immortal by allowing him to take a sip of the elixir of youth and longevity, Amrita, which he had obtained from the Mighty Garuda after the majestic bird of prey had rescued his mother Vinata.

Having thus acquired the status of immortality, Shasandevtas, projected himself on to the planet of the rakshashas (giants), the sons and daughters of Krodhavasha who had the ability to assume the likeness of mortal men and women.

The planet itself was covered in eternal twilight and when rakshashas projected themselves to other worlds or travelled via starships to other planets; it's the hour that they are most potent.

Being shapes shifters they were gifted with the ability to assume any form or shape that they wished and they were free to mimic any being in the universe including cosmic and celestial entities.

When he first projected himself the rakshashas tried to devour him but because Shasandevtas had acquired the gift of immortality, he was able to withstand the repeated attacks of the rakshashas. Finally, the rakshashas gave up and accepted him as one of their own and eventually conferred upon him the ability to alter his form.

Shasandevtas returned to the mortal world after taking a raksha wife. His descendants are known as Yasnas and Yasnis or (male fairies and female fairies) and because they come from his bloodline, they share his gifts.

Members of this now extinct Sect though mortal acquired the power to alter their sizes and those that remain reside in the celestial Kingdom of Indra.

The most ferocious of the magical creatures is a creature called Narashima or a man-beast that is half man and half lion. The Sect is devoted to the worship of Narashima the half man half lion God. They are descendants of the God who was initially incarnated to defeat the Demon Hiranyakashipu. The Demon by virtue of having acquired a boon was impervious to attacks by any mortal, beast or God and he set about ravaging and plundering the mortal world. The positive aspect of the Brahmatma assumed a form that was neither God, man or beast and manifested itself as Narashima to defeat Hiranyakashipu.

The forested areas during the battle before time were rife with not only elves, dwarfs, unicorns, centaurs, hayagrivas and narashimas but they were also alive with yakshas who lived in mountains and forests. Yakshas were the servant warriors of the God of wealth Kubera and protected the garden located at the base of Mount Kaylas. The surface below the garden was laden with treasures as were the caves which were storage facilities for treasure troves.

Despite their indisputable strength, they were peaceful creatures that co-existed harmoniously with both mortals and other magical creatures and at times were even of service to them.

Kubera ruled over the highlands of the Betan Plateau and his capital was located in the magnificent and majestic city of Alaka, which was also known as the city of a thousand lakes. The lakes of Alaka were adrift with lotuses and teeming with shoals of white swans.

The palace of Kubera was located in the highest precinct of the city. It was built of pure gold and adorned with gemstones with towers so high that they almost touched the sky.

Kubera's preferred form is that of a one eyed giant with three stumpy legs and a huge pot belly. Despite his uncomely appearance he is an immensely popular God with mortals because of his ability to bestow wealth but despite the overwhelming mortal following he chose his loyal body-guards to be the benefactors of his Sect because yakshas did not value gold. Instead they measured wealth in terms of courage and to Kubera the yakshas were worth their weight in gold.

The ritualistic rites and traditions observed by the Sects vary from Sect to Sect and included in the classification of Sects were the occult Sects and as stipulated by occult sciences their ceremonies are conducted during the bewitching hours i.e. between midnight and dawn. Pivotal among the occult Sects is the Sect of Veetal (bat), and as transcribed and prescribed by the elders of the Sect all rites and rituals of the Sect use the elixir of life, blood, as a conduit to summon their Goddess.

The Sect of Veetal is in essence and substance a vampire Sect and members of the Sect are the offspring of the occupants of the night and stray away from the light of sun. That however does not mean that they cannot appear in broad daylight. To the contrary, those that belong in the higher echelons of the Sect or have been conferred the title of "elder" are impervious to the scorching rays of the sun.

The Sect remained in seclusion and was unknown to most and their existence only came to light during the reign of King Vikramaditya, the son of Gandharba-Sena the donkey and the daughter of the King of Dhara. At birth Vikramaditya was granted the strength of a thousand elephants by his father.

When his sire died, his grandfather, Indra, resolved that the child should not be born and upon hearing the news, his mother stabbed herself and succumbed to the wounds. The tragic event however occurred in the ninth month and the arrival of Vikramaditya heralded the death of his mother. The child was delivered to Indra, who despite his initial reluctance took to the boy and raised him to be a king of the highest stature and caliber.

On the morn of each day Vikramaditya seated on his throne of power and opulence granted an audience to all mortals regardless of their status and demeanor in society and on this particular day, he was approached by a mendicant. He did not ask for alms but instead presented the king with a fruit and retreated.

Vikramaditya not wanting to the offend the beggar in anyway received the fruit and just as he was about to hand it to his courtier, his pet monkey, attempted to wrest the pomegranate away from him and in the friendly joust that ensued the fruit fell to the ground. As the fruit struck the hard wood paneled floor it shattered and fragmented into thousands of invaluable rubies.

Vikramaditya shocked and stunned at what he had witnessed immediately sent his servant after the beggar to ask him to return. The young man ran after the mendicant and told him that the king would like to speak to him again and asked if the mendicant would return and the mendicant consented to do so.

"What manner of magic is this?" asked Vikramaditya. "It is the magic of the Aghori Sect dear king" replied the mendicant and "what you have seen is merely the tip of the iceberg, mere objects, as opposed to the untapped riches that you can have, should you so desire" he continued. Intrigued the king asked "how can I acquire this knowledge?". The mendicant bowed his head and replied, you have to follow me to the cemetery in which I reside.

Vikramaditya agreed and followed the mendicant to the cremation grounds where the mendicant resided. The mendicant led him to the spot of a freshly extinguished cremation pyre, the remains still fresh on the charred ground and sat cross legged on the blackened ashes that were sprawled on the surface.

He then instructed Vikramaditya to do the same and commenced with the ritual to transfer the knowledge that he had promised to the king. Just as he was about to complete the telepathic transfer he said to the king "in order to complete the rite, I need the body of a female that hangs downwards from the branches of a tree like a bat does from the roof of a cave" he said. "Where will I find such a corpse?" asked Vikramaditya. "You will find her hanging down from the boughs of the banyan tree that occupy the fringes of this graveyard" he replied.

"You have to bring the corpse back to me but it has to be done between the hours of midnight and dawn" continued the mendicant. "But be warned, noble Vikramaditya, under no circumstances are you allowed to talk to the veetal (vampire)" he said.

Vikramaditya nodded his head and at the appointed hour left in search of the corpse and approximately three hours later at the stroke of three, the hour of occult rites, he found that which he was seeking.

He was taken aback by what he saw. The corpse that was hanging down from the bough of the tree, was that of a young maiden, her skin as pale as snow and as smooth and as languid as the ice that covered the tops of a lake in winter. She looked untainted and unsoiled, the surface of her skin appeared untouched by mortal hands, her lips as red as blood, that dripped from an open vein.

Vikramaditya faltered and stumbled but eventually composed himself as he walked towards the corpse, the scent from its golden hair filled his nostrils with the sweet aroma of wild jasmine. He lifted the weightless corpse down effortlessly before slinging it across his shoulders and making his way back to the ashes of the funeral pyre.

On the way back the vampire started speaking to the king, its voice soft and melodic like that of a seasoned minstrel and the king soon drifted into a dreamy trance. He found himself in a cobblestone paved courtyard surrounded by citadels capped with golden domes. He stood in front of the sultry vampire and she opened her eyelids to reveal eyes the color of shimmering sapphire.

Vikramaditya stood still, rooted to the ground, his limbs frozen, taken aback, by her enchanting beauty. The veetal laughed and the puzzled king asked "why do you laugh?" and he was instantly brought back to the present. The corpse left his shoulders and drifted back through the air and clung once again, feet up to the bough of the banyan tree.

Vikramaditya, remember the words of the mendicant and shook his head ruefully for speaking. He repeated the exercise and yet again the vampire tricked him into speaking. Finally, after the sixth attempt, the vampire tired and spoke thus to the king. "You tire me with your wasteful efforts. Now let me now tell you some stories to amuse you".

The Veetal told the Vikramaditya fifteen tales of wisdom that became the cornerstones of the Vampire Sect and those associated with them: -

- ❖ Vampires and their associates are blessed with clairvoyant dreams.
- ❖ Vampires exist in broods or clans and they work in unison to accomplish their tasks.
- ❖ Vampires are immune to attacks by swords, blades, daggers and other sharp implements.
- ❖ Vampires are immune from death by beheadings.
- ❖ Vampires have the ability to resurrect themselves after cremation and therefore are not subject to death by fire. In truth fire reduces their bodies to ashes but as soon as the fire is quenched vampires resurrect themselves.
- ❖ The skin of the vampire is always smooth and un-faltered. It is immune to cuts, abrasions, burns and other conditions that afflict mortal skin.
- ❖ Vampires and those associated to them abstain from the ritual of sacrifice.
- ❖ Vampires abstain from using black, their preferred color is white.
- ❖ Vampires have the ability to invade the dreams of others though in practice this is only done by the succubus who is the dark equivalent of the vampire and the clan of the succubus ascribes to the negative aspect of the Brahmatma.

- ❖ All vampires abide by an oath of fidelity and loyalty.
- ❖ Vampires do not age.
- ❖ Vampires do not have a reflection.
- ❖ Vampires do not cast a shadow.
- ❖ Vampires subsist on the nectar of fruits and flowers from the valley. The elixir of life, blood, merely prologues their continuity and blood is only consumed on the night of the full moon. Should the vampire forgo the rite of the blood feed, it will return to mortality and eventually lose all its vampire traits.
- ❖ The blood of the vampire is a powerful elixir and if consumed it will reward those who have been blessed to taste its blood with the traits of the vampire.

I have thus outlined the laws governing the Vampire Sect simple because they still walk among us and have proved in the past to be valuable allies in our struggle against the forces of evil that seek to coerce and enslave all mortality.

Towards the end, the vampire, a creature of unparalleled beauty revealed to the king the deviant design of the sorcerer who planned to kill the king once the vampire was delivered to him. His only intention was to obtain the blood of the vampire and by consuming its blood acquire the gift of immortality.

Vikramaditya having thus been warned killed the sorcerer and as soon as he returned to the funeral pyre. He removed the sorcerer's head from his shoulders with a single stroke of his mighty sword.

In addition to vampires there were also Gandharvas. Gandharvas are male deities who are surrounded by an aura of flames. They reside in the sky and are often construed as being spirits of fire and aether. Like Apsaras they are gifted with magical powers but do not have the vested power to control the elements and are often simply referred to as the minstrels of heaven. Their tasks include preparing the elixir of immortality, Amrita, obtained from the soma fruit that grows in the garden of heaven.

The Gandharvas were born of Brahma and were the result of the imbibing melody that he sang in honor of the Goddess Gayathri filled with love, passion and exuberance. Chitraratha is the God of the Gandharvas because he is the first born of the Gandharvas and presides over all the cities of the Gandharvas. I can safely say that these cities are splendid beyond description or comprehension. The Gandharvas Sect comprises entirely of males.

The female equivalent of Gandhavas are Dakinis and they are gifted with the ability to manipulate the weather. The Sect of Dakini is presided over by the Goddess Varahi the female incarnate of Vishnu's boar avatar, and the entire Sect like that of their male counterparts comprises entirely of females.

Varahi rarely appears in depictions because only a few have seen her. With the exception of those who are gifted with insurmountable amount of talent, like the Demon Slayer Mägi, she is virtually unknown.

While many would regard the presence of a boar's head on the shoulders of a woman as abhorrent, the Goddess in reality is of exceptional beauty and her beguiling appearance is a warning to others not to approach her temples. The Gandharvas Sect and the Dakini Sect are also classified as occult Sects and thus the ritual of summoning is conducted between the hours of midnight and dawn.

Dakinis are of exceptionally beauty and they are the spiritual consorts of the most valiant warriors. Their mortal body is of little significance to them. Though they are born with the mortal frame of the sultry temptresses, they quickly gain or achieve the ability to free their soul from their body and stray or steer towards the elements.

It is not unknown for valiant warriors to wed Dakinis. The Demon Slayer Mägi wedded the Dakini Lukina and mortals who desire wealth and power often conjugate with Dakinis. It is not unheard of for mortal men, at the request of a Dakini, to slay her mortal body thus freeing the soul forever and making the Dakini his spiritual consort.

Such a mortal will be rewarded with immense wealth and power but he must visit the Dakini every night and he is forbidden from acquiring mortal lovers for Dakinis are extremely possessive and it is not unknown for them to instigate the demise of wayward partners.

It is however permissible for mortals to have more than one spiritual consort or lover, with the permission of the other, of course. Finally, though this list is not exhaustive, there are the Maruts whose skin is as black as tar. The Maruts are an inter-mediatory race who were born during the great battle.

Diti, the progenitor of the Demon Clan was disturbed to see her children suffer and she drifted into transcendental sleep in search of the sage Kashyapa to request a boon. She navigated through the corridors of the super-consciousness and when she found him she asked for a son powerful enough to slay Indra.

Kashyapa accordingly directed Ditti to go on a holy pilgrimage to a place called Syamantapanchaka and upon her arrival she was instructed to constructed a rudimentary hut and subsist on a diet of wild fruits and milk for a thousand years.

Diti did as she was told and isolated herself for a thousand mortal years. Her prayers pleased Kashyapa and he granted her a boon as a result of her piousness. "Please grant me a son who will kill Indra" she asked. "It shall be as you wish" said Kashyapa in response to her request. "But there are certain conditions that you need to fulfill. You will be confined to this hermitage for a thousand years and you will have to carry the baby in your womb for the duration of the thousand years. In addition to that, there are certain other conditions that you need to fulfill. You must be extremely clean and you must not eat in the evening, nor must you sleep under a tree at night. Neither is any form of exercise permitted" he added.

"Do not sleep with your hair unbraided or without having had a bath. If you can righteously observe these rules for a thousand mortal years, you will have the that son you wish for" he continued.

Diti agreed and the apparition that was Kashyapa dissolved into thin air. The rules in effect surrounded Diti with an invisible protective shield that Indra could not breach unless the Kashyapa's stipulations were broken. Diti began to observe the rites that the sage had prescribed as soon he disappeared but Indra realized that something was afoot and he wasn't about the permit the birth of a child that would eventually orchestrate his demise be born.

He disguised himself as humble forlorn woodcutter and started delivering firewood to Diti's doorstep. He brought her fruits from the valley and the nectar of wild bees. He tended to the cows that grazed in the pastures nearby, milking them daily for Diti's sustenance. In reality however, he was waiting for the right moment so that he could strike and deliver a deadly blow.

Ninety-nine hundred years passed in this manner and three days prior to delivery Diti grew weary. Secure in the thought that she had almost completed her ordeal, she let her concentration lapse and she went to bed without washing her hair and left it unbraided and unbridled.

Indra seized the opportunity. By not abiding by the rules that had been stipulated by Kashyapa, Diti had lowered her defenses and the protective shield that Kashyapa had conferred upon her was now breach-able. Indra entered Diti's womb in a flash armed with a vajra, a sharp celestial weapon which doubled up as club, because of the strength of its blade.

With the vajra, Indra sliced the baby in Diti's womb into seven parts but because the baby was almost mature, the parts were alive and began to wince and cry in pain. Indra in an attempt to stifle the noise continued to carve away at the parts and eventually he ended up with forty-nine different parts.

Since Diti had failed to observe the prescribed rites, the forty-nine parts were no longer a threat to Indra and when they were born they became known as the Maruts. Indra compelled by the wails of the infant Maruts and to atone for his sin elevated the Maruts to the status of Demigods and they became Indra's friends and companions.

The Maruts all forty-nine of them because of their unconventional birth were restlessness by nature and violent in action. Indra blessed them with powers to instigate strong winds and precipitate savage storms. The Maruts became synonymous and analogous to winds, storms, and torrential rain that belted and pelted the land with overwhelming force.

Diti did not succeed in her attempt to kill Indra simply because Indra cannot be killed. He is constant and perpetual and remains throughout the fourteen Manvantras. He endures for the eight point six-four billion years of the universe.

The Grand Empire

The first emperor of the Grand Empire Vishvamitra, a descendent of the solar deities, was propelled to the exulted position by the nine dakinis he coupled with every night. In addition to being his consorts, they were also his principle advisors and with their help he laid the foundations for the biggest contiguous empire ever built in the mortal world which included, citadels, palaces, forts and canals that were unequalled and unrivaled in design and precision.

Dakinis had the ability to not only control the temporal weather but to also to alter and redirect the flow of water, an ability that their male counterparts Gandhavas did not have and with their help he was able to irrigate inhospitable terrain and facilitate agriculture.

The Goddess Anapoorna, Goddess of Grains, gave him the seven grains that became the staple food of the empire, to sow. The seven grains were rice, wheat, corn, barley, sorghum, oats and rye to cultivate on the now fertile lands.

Bhumi, Goddess of Earth churned the soil and the decomposed matter, the flesh and the bones of mortals, Demons and magical creatures that remained hidden between layers of earth and gravel surfaced to nourish the soil. Nandi the white bull of heaven descended from Mt. Kailash, the abode of Shiva, and gifted him with strong oxen to pull the plough, that was given to him by the Goddess of Ploughs, Saranya.

The air was rife with white magic and all persons were in touch with their super-consciousness. The odorless, gaseous matter was so strong that one could almost touch it. Vishvamitra had nine sons for each Dakini bequeathed him a son. The eldest became his successor and the other eight were granted territories in each of the eight directions of the compass and were instructed to expand their holdings by either guile or conquest. It was under his guidance that the Sects became organized and the Sectarian Council was formed. It was the time of my first birth in the present universe and of all the countless births I have had later it is the birth that I was the fondest of.

I was born into my Sect and in time I was appointed leader of my Sect. It was after my marriage that troubled loomed over the horizon and sounds of swords clashing against shields blared ominously in distant lands. The sons of Vishvamitra after colonizing much of the untamed lands and uniting the various Sects had reached the fringes of the Central Kingdoms.

The duality of existence encompassed all things and like the conscious mind and the subconscious mind, like the physical body and the soul, that are inseparable yet separable, good and evil likewise have an un-intelligible nexus.

It was a semi-arid desolate land adorned with buildings made from red earthen bricks and crowned with golden domes. It was a land where men dressed in soft lose fitting shirts and baggy pants and had scimitars strapped to their sides.

Among all the citadels that the visitors stumbled across there was one taller than the rest its triangular dome was shaped and crafted from the blazing red gold of Demons and ornamented with precious stones.

The temple had existed since the formation of the earth, when soil and gravel had rose to the top. Bhumi had touched the surface with her dainty fingers and enriched the soil with nutrients.

The temple had burrowed its way to the surface through the topsoil and steadily increased in height until it stood taller than any building that could be feasibly contrived by mortal hands. It looked pure and immaculate, untouched and unsoiled and appeared to be in mint condition. The locals called it the Temple of Ahriman or the Temple of Dark Matter for that is what the name Ahriman means - dark matter.

The unfortunate son of Vishvamitra who stumbled across the temple was Adhanya. He ferried his troops across the rugged hostile terrain, bearing the hawk symbol of the Empire on his bronze breastplates. From the records of the scribes that accompanied Adhanya, the journey was nothing but smooth partly attributed to the vast quantities of white magic that remained in the air carried over from the time of creation.

Adhanya was taken in by the monumental structure and succumbed to its charms the moment he set eyes on the glistening roof that was visible like a shining beacon on a moonless night. He was instantly drawn to it, captivated by its magnetic charms; he led his army of archers and horse lancers towards it. As they reigned closer, the dirt and gravel path that they trod and trampled on gave way to a track paved with cobblestone.

They soon reached a wide open courtyard with a fountain powered by ox-driven pumps surrounded by brown ridden shrubbery that more than adequately made up for the lack of trees. The explicit heat made the men sweat beneath their metal armor.

According to the scribes the courtyard was deserted and facing the pool was an arched entrance that led towards the interior of the temple. The walls of the temple were formed from black marble and the floor was paved in geometrical fashion with octagonal stars that alternated with cruciform shapes.

The interior of the temple was abuzz with the stilled sound of silence and despite the relentless heat; it was cool, filled with the ambiance of twilight.

Along the walls, spaced out, were huge vases that were filled with rare flowers like tulips, irises, daffodils, and narcissus that filled the air with an opulent scent. Semi-precious stones shaped in the fashion of twining vines, fruits, and flowers were pressed delicately into the marble walls.

Right in the middle of what was evidently a large chamber stood a stone sarcophagus and on it, brazenly emboldened on the sides were depictions of men in crafts that sailed through infinite space. The scribes that accompanied Adhanya into the chamber deduced that it was an inter-stellar map that revealed the location of the person or the object that was entombed in the sarcophagus.

The scribes recorded that they felt a sudden urge to walk towards the sarcophagus and as they did so vivid images of a huge ship traversing the stars flashed through before them.

Adhanya stood like a man in a trance. He inched closer tentatively. The others did the same and as they moved closer, it began to glow. He reached over to the coffin and pushed the lid open with both his hands and if they expected any resistance there was none. Instead it felt warm and welcoming.

They pushed the lid aside and the men gathered around, milling like sheep, to look inside it and all they could see was a dark empty space lit by the light of shimmering stars. They pulled away afraid that they might fall into it and stared blankly as a dark cloud drifted upwards from within and soon towered above them.

The cloud began to take shape and soon changed and altered to display the shape of a man, thin, tall and deviously handsome. The surface of his skin was pale and languid, soft and untainted like that of a vampire and his longish face stood haughtily on a pair of broad shoulders. His hair was as black as a raven and reached down to his neck. His eyes were ablaze with torrid red flames. He was dressed completely in black and he glared at them with his blazing eyes. Adhanya and his men fell instantly under the hypnotic spell that flared from his blaring eyes.

There was only one person who made it back, the rest remained transfixed in the Central Kingdoms. He brought with him the scrolls that recorded the journey which he submitted to Vishvamitra before taking his life with his own blade.

The will of Ahriman, the very incarnate of evil had turned him, like it turned the others when they looked into his inferno like eyes. According to the scrolls black magic oozed out from within the sarcophagus and soon defiled and polluted the air, thinning it with its noxious and toxic touch causing the white magic that was in the air to dissipate.

Men and beast got their first glimpse of darkness and from within the sarcophagus Ahriman brought forward hordes and legions of deviantly twisted and perverse creatures that seeped into the territories of the other sons of Vishvamitra.

Thus began the Battle before Time and Adhanya led the forces of the Central Kingdoms after uniting the fragmented and disfranchised tribes that once roamed freely on its luscious fertile plains.

He was eventually crowned the first king of the Central Kingdoms. The forces of light united under the banner of the Great God Ahura Mazda, the living incarnate of white matter, who appeared in person to lead the forces of good against his arch nemesis, Ahriman, Lord Protector and Lord Preceptor of Darkness.

All magical creatures have their equivalent that worshipped the negative aspect of the Brahmatma. Elves for example have as their nemesis dark elves a morbid spawn of cohesive mating between white elves and Demons by the loathsome forces of Ahriman. Towards the end of the battle many of the magical creatures became extinct and shunned the world of mortals seeking residence in hidden forests, subterranean caves, below watery expanses and some ventured to distant planets and other worlds.

The Living Goddess

B efore I go further I think it is only proper that I mention briefly at least, not that the she needs any introduction, the life force of Hawk's Nest, the living embodiment of all our prayers, the Living Goddess who is none other than the personification of the Guardian of the Universe, the female manifestation of Vishnu, she who is known only as the Living Goddess, she who is of immaculate conception.

The female avatar of Vishnu (Durga) is the most potent of all goddesses because she embodies all the qualities of the Brahmatma associated with the conservation and preservation of life including war and she is known, despite being worshipped as Durga, only as Vaishnavi. Vaishnavi was born, as was I, in the semi-arid lands of the south. Before her birth, her mortal father, a sage of some note and moderate means and her mortal mother a devoted worshiper of the Solar Deities went childless for many years.

After performing severe austerities and after years of rigorous and relentless worship, Brahma appeared before the sage, whose name was Ratnakar and granted him a boon. Ratnakar requested for a child and Brahma consented but on the condition that the child be allowed to do as she wished. The sage agreed and Vaishnavi was conceived.

The young Vaishnavi being from the lineage of Vishnu and Durga was a free spirited child, who refused to be shackled by the chains of customs and traditions. Being gifted with the natural ability to tap into the vaults of the subconscious mind, she was able to access the knowledge of the ages and was able to transport herself to the future where she caught a glimpse of her husband who was none other than an avatar of Vishnu. The young Vaishnavi foresaw a dark cloud loom above the mortal world and in order to save mortality from the clutches of Ahriman she made her way to the shores of the eastern sea and there she went into transcendental sleep.

Centuries passed and the sound of silence that resonated from within her small frame, the sound of creation, aum, reached Vishnu's consciousness and in response the Great Enchantress, the Devi Mahatmaya appeared before her, in the form of her future husband.

The great enchantress approached Vaishnavi and as the soles of her feet touched the golden sand of the seashore, Vaishnavi raised her eyelids, sensing her presences. The instant the young girl saw the Devi in the form of her husband, Vaishnavi spoke. Vaishnavi told the warrior (the enchantress in disguise) that she wished to marry him. The warrior smiled and told the young girl that she had to wait patiently until it was time for the next avatar of Vishnu to step on to the mortal world.

In the meantime, the warrior instructed her to wait for him in a cave located in the Forbidden Mountains. There under the watchful eyes of the father of the mountains, Markendaya and his nine daughters, she who we venerate as the Living Goddess waits patiently for her beloved.

The whereabouts of the cave that she resides in is known only to me and I do not choose to reveal its location at present but I will reveal something of its nature for those who chance to stumble across it by accident. The shrine, the home of the Living Goddess, is deceiving in appearance and appears to be nothing more than an ordinary cave embossed with rock and sediment.

Before entering the cave, one must first gain the favor of Chandi and to gain the favor of Chandi one must first appease the Demons Shumba and Nisumba, battle the Demon Mahishasura, and overcome the Demons Madhu and Kaitabha. Their decapitated heads are buried three feet from her shrine below the gravel. The entrance to the cave is only accessible at noon, when the Demons are at their weakest and they are out to feed. It is the most feasible time to enter the cave where Vaishnavi is in meditative sleep. Being omniscient and omnipresent, she is able to project herself and to be in many places at the same time.

The Dron Shamans

Prior to what has now become a battle for survival, the gates between the worlds had been opened and a new faith that was neither a friend nor foe of Ahriman had emerged and was allowed to fester. It was known as shamanism. Its founder was a young man who had been abducted and transported to the nether regions where he was taught the secrets of Demons.

Dron is the original faith of the people of the Betan Plateau. It is a realization and an admittance that we share this world with others, some visible and some not. Ancient but not obsolete, it is a faith that's still practiced, handed down through the years, often merged with Tantric teachings.

The Tantric Sects form the smallest group in the Sectarian hierarchy but they have far reaching influences. There are in total ten Tantric Sects each under the auspice of a separate Goddess. Collectively they hold in their folds the occult knowledge of the universe. They are entirely occult in nature and their rites and rituals as per the norm with all occult Sects are performed during the hours of midnight and dawn.

The Tantric Sects are more contemporary than their predecessors the Vedic Sects and therefore are not accorded a place in the Sectarian Council. The formation of these Sects occurred during the great battle and if it wasn't for their help, all would have been lost. There is no particular order to the Sects and therefore I will start with the most predominant Tantric Sect, that of the Tantric Goddess Kali.

The name Kali means killer of time or devourer of time and the Sect of Kali like their most auspicious Goddess immerse themselves in black and perform Tantric rites that are spurned by the more orthodox Vedic Sects.

During the Battle Before Time, the forces of Ahriman unleashed a ferocious Demon called Raktabija whose decapitated head lies buried beneath the rock cut foundation of the Temple of Kali.

Raktabija was gifted a boon and in accordance with the boon a new Demon appears from any drop of blood that spills to ground from the body of Raktabija. The forces of darkness set the Demon loose on the mortal world and it rampaged and ravaged its way through the defenses of the Empire.

The eight sons of the Vishvamitra were at a loss when their defenses were blunted by the Demon and defeat looked imminent. They summoned the leaders of the Sects and collectively they used their mental energies to sift through the infinite knowledge that is stored in the super-consciousness for a God, Goddess or Divinity who was capable of defeating Raktabija and they soon stumbled across a planet the was dark and cold.

It was an isolated planet so distant from the stars that light never touched its surface and there seated on a golden throne on a floor constructed from the ivory bones of Demons wearing a garland of skulls with blood dripping from the sides of her mouth, siting naked and cross legged was the Goddess Kali.

The leaders of the Sects summoned her and upon hearing their laments, the great huntress streaked across the cosmos like a blazing comet and landed with a sound so loud that it was heard in every precinct of the mortal world.

Armed with a sword on her right hand and a solar disc in her left hand that she sent veering though the air to severe the heads of Demons from their bodies, she went to battle Raktabija. She cut and hacked at the ferocious Demon but unlike the others before her who could not stop his blood from dripping to the ground, Kali savored each drop of blood which oozed from the Demon's body lapping it up with her tongue and the contaminated blood of the Demon sent her into an ecstatic frenzy that bordered on sheer ecstasy.

Unable to replicate, the Demon drained of the elixir of life, capitulated and the Goddess severed the head off the grotesque body after sucking the body dry of blood. She took the head back to the spot where she first landed and buried it beneath the soil. A temple was later erected on the ground above to honor the Goddess.

Having failed in their attempt to fill the mortal world with replicate Raktibija's, the forces of darkness conspired to eliminate the mortal race again. The Demons attacked in multitudes and soon usurped the Sect of Varuna, the guardians of oceans, seas, rivers and waterways and gained control of all surface water which they churned into a noxious poison that was deadly to the mortal physique.

Indra who wielded the thousand knotted thunderbolt went forth to battle the Demons and unleashed volley upon volley of unrepentant lighting that struck the Demons repeatedly from all directions but the Demons neither flinched nor faltered.

Vishvamitra fraught with worry and unable to contain the threat any longer approached Shiva for help. Shiva came down from Mt. Kailash seated on the white bull of heaven Nandi and consumed all the surface water on the planet before churning the water in his belly separating the poison from drinkable water and spitting it out again but the Demons remorselessly continued with the unrepentant attack and Shiva feel ill from the residue of the poison that remained in his body and fainted. His skin glowed with a tainted bluish hue.

The powers of creation convened and the merciful Tara appeared in the mortal world for the first time. She nursed Shiva back to health before assuming a wrathful posture and in a battle that lasted for the duration of a single night flayed the Demons, slicing them to pieces with her sword of seven splendors.

Following the defeat, the Demon Clan resorted to guile and craft to forge a victory and targeted the leader of the Aghora Sect while he was in meditative sleep exploring the unlimited realm of the super-consciousness to acquire spells and that had long been forgotten to strengthened the grip the Aghori Sect had on mortals.

The Demons enlisted the help of Kama, a pint sized god with angelic wings attached to his back who was armed with a sugarcane bow and arrows of love. Kama was a delightful lad who fluttered about like a wild butterfly with blonde curls and eyes as blue as the sky. A free spirited God, Kama had thus far refused to take sides in the war and Ahriman's emissaries approached him with a proposition most suited to his gentle demure.

Ahriman made him an offer he could not refuse. He would allow Kama to work his magic of love and lust in the Central Kingdoms if he could get Aghora smitten with a strike of his arrow. The jovial God readily agreed and he approached Aghora who was seated cross-legged in meditative sleep on the ashes of a funeral pyre. Just as Kama was about to loosen his shaft Aghora opened his middle eye and an intense ray hotter than the blazing sun burst forth reducing Kama to ashes within the blink of an eye.

Aghora perturbed by the attack discontinued his meditation and departed for the planet Aghoram giving what had transpired no thought, dismissing it as matter little significance or consequence.

The emissaries of Ahriman however were not so hasty, and having anticipated the demise of Kama, they lurked around and gathered the ashes of the God, from which they molded a fearsome figurine. They infused it with dark matter and in a space of days it grew in dimensions and soon reached the proportions of a full grown Demon. The called the Demon Bhandasura.

Bhandasura, ignored the material pleasures of the mortal world and denied himself the joys of interstellar travel. Instead the Demon absolved himself of all sin by being a devout and austere worshiper of Shiva and in time the God with the matted dreadlocks responded kindly to the Demon and granted him a boon.

Bhandasura's request was simply that any opponent that stood against him would lose half his strength and that portion of strength would go to Bhandasura. Shiva consented and Bhandasura energized by his newly acquired powers savagely ravaged the mortal world.

From the remaining ashes of Kama, Bhandasura shaped two other dolls Vishukra and Vishanga and infused the pair with dark matter. They became brothers of Bhandasura and they in turn forged other Demons from Kama's ashes and soon a Demon horde of unprecedented strength came into existence. The forces of light were once again confronted with a perplexing enemy that they couldn't apprehend, confine, contain or destroy.

The forces of light summoned the collective powers of the Sects and they entered transcendental sleep, a meditative state that gifted them with the ability to travel through time and space and guided by the positive powers of the Brahmatma they stumbled across the city of the Goddess Lalitha located on a distance world build from an alloy of two metals (iron, silver) and three gemstones (diamond, sapphire and onyx). There, seated on an ornamental throne of ivory was the daughter of Lalitha, Shodashi, who was no older than sixteen and Vishvamitra himself knelt before her and pleaded for her help. Shodashi kindly consented and she departed with her army to confront the Demon horde.

Her army was commanded by Dhandini who rode on a chariot called Giri Chakra and Manthrini who rode on a chariot called Geya Chakra. Jwala Malini protected the army by creating a ring of fire around it.

Lalita Shodashi herself rode in the center on her bejeweled chariot, her troops holding the lines in the formation of a Chakra. Nithya, the eternal, general extraordinaire, destroyed a large chunk of Bandasura's armies, Anima killed the son of Bandasura, and Manthrini and Dhandini disposed of Vishanga and Vishukra.

The Demons then created a blockade to stop the marching army and Mahima with the help of Kameshwara removed the blockade.

It was an epic battle, of two well-armed and well-equipped contingents and a ferocious battle ensued. Lalitha cut and hacked her way through the battlefield and eventually cleaved her way to victory.

The fourth goddess in the Tantric echelon is Bhuvaneshwari whose Sect is an intermediary Sect. In the Tantric circle, it is not forbidden to draw upon the negative powers of the Brahmatma and as one dives deeper into the rites and rituals of the Tantric Sects one would realize or discover that Tantrics call upon the powers of both light and darkness but have acquired the ability to keep the forces of darkness at bay or in shackles and as such Tantric prowess becomes exceedingly relevant to shamans. With the help of Tantric deities' shamans can bind and harness the energies of darkness and channel it to suit their purpose and achieve their designs.

The palace of the Bhuvaneshwari is located on a planet, that unlike most planets does not revolve on a fictional axis. The first half of the planet is covered in light while the other half of the planet is covered in darkness and it remains motionless.

Half of her palace is located in the precinct lit by the light of a sun and the other half of her palace is located in a precinct that is continually and continuously engulfed in darkness. The Sect of the Goddess likewise co-exists mutually with both the powers of light and darkness and territories governed by the Sect of Bhuvaneshwari are often accorded the status of being neutral.

The Demons enraged at successive defeats summoned the Demon hordes of Rahu, a Demon that was a serpent below the belly. It sat astride a chariot pulled by eight black horses and was accompanied by legions of fierce Demons, that descended from the sky in a gash of blinding light ripping through the dark cauldron night, cutting and hacking their way while balefire red blood oozed and splattered from the open wounds of mortals and magical creatures.

Celestial beings fled in terror from their heavenly abodes and the waterways were clogged by thick molten red blood as the Demons pounded and pummeled mortal defenses under a canopy of stars.

Struck by a swarms of arrows, blizzards of spears and a tempest of lances, Vishvamitra's armies were sent rasping and keening through the blizzard black night. The forces of light faltered and were soon trampled and flattened by the onslaught, their bones ground to dust, and scattered to the four corners of the mortal world by the eerie wind that accompanied the distressed wailing of the fallen.

Those that remained gripped their gelid swords with their cold hands, while the blood of their companions splashed and splattered across their faces. They watched haplessly as the blood oozed out from the sluiced wounds. The battle raged for days and it appeared all would be lost but the Sects remained steadfast and summoned the Goddess who is at home among broken bodies, splattered remains and pools of blood.

Her name was Chinnamasta and she is the Goddess Divine of the Headless Sect, whose members are summoned often by shamans of the Betan Plateau to strike fear and terror into the hearts of their enemies.

From the ember ground she appeared, her hair a flaming red, beneath the profane sky, unclothed and naked, her luscious breasts swaying and swaggering in the heat of battle. Overcome by blood lust, she cleaved her head off her shoulders and blood spurted from the gaping stump falling to the ground. She rushed at the enemy mangling and gashing at their serried ranks, cutting and hacking with both her hands, armed with a sword and a cleaver.

The headless Goddess stood boldly before the Demons and thinned their ranks. The sordid bodies of the wicked littered the battlefield. Sensing defeat, Ragu fled the mortal world back to his home planet that was filled with noxious gases with temperatures hundreds of degrees below zero.

The remaining Demons withdrew but not before they cast a spell to preserve the rotting bodies in the decomposing state and soon the stench of death and decay permeated the air. Mortal bodies were too frail to withstand the toxic effects of the noxious stench and many became ill, falling prey to a sudden plague that swept through the empire like a lackluster wind carrying with it the smell of rot.

The Sects were forced to summon the aid of Bhairavi who lived on a planet littered with rotting carcasses from all corners of the universe. Remains that wouldn't decompose by natural means were sent to her planet and the Goddess with the powers conferred to her by the Brahmatma accelerated decay. Decomposition and degeneration are essential to the continuity of the universe and should either cease the universe would come to a standstill and souls will remain trapped within rotting carcasses.

The intolerable putrid stench of death filled the air. The Goddess whose eyes blazed with the fires of a thousand cremation pyres with a single look could set any corpse alight reducing it to ashes within minutes and replace the pungent, nauseating stench of rot with the scented fragrance of the cremation fires.

Her skin was as black as charred ashes and her hair was long, matted ad disheveled. The skin on her body was wrinkled, creased and crumpled like the surface of a discarded prune and her teeth were a stained yellow.

The leaders of Sects projected themselves to the surface of the planet littered with languid corpses that the Goddess called home and scavenged its surface for her presence. Once they had found her, they bowed at her feet and pleaded for her help and the Goddess magnanimously consented to aiding them with the stipulation that her Sect be allowed to exist unhindered and unencumbered in the mortal world.

The Sect Leaders consented. The agreement concluded, she appeared in the mortal world. The cremation fires burst forth from her eyes and reduced the carcasses to smoldering ashes. Fueled by the rage of Agni and the righteousness of Mainyu Athra, the flames fed on the decapitated corpses that lay sprawling on the ground and blazed like a towering inferno that could be seen from distant planets.

I will now reveal that which is only known to those who belong to the higher echelons of the Vedic Sects. The Sect of Bhairavi is gifted with the ability to breathe life into corpses and make them do their bidding.

As long as the body is not reduced to ashes or dust, the soul remains trapped within it and with the aid of mantras that are known only to those who belong to the inner sanctum of the sect, the corpses may be brought back to life. This is the ability that the Shamans of the Betan Plateau seek when they approach the Goddess for her aid and assistance.

Having failed in their attempts to bring the Grand Empire to its knees, Adhanya, with the help of Ahriman travelled to the planet Aghoram, a planet that was filled with ash, soot and the charred remains from cremation pyres around the universe. It was a planet lit by the light of ten visible moons, to seek the help of Aghora, Lord Preceptor of the Aghori Sect.

Adhanya found a suitable pyre that was still ablaze and with the help of Ahriman's black magic, he sat himself on the burning fire, untouched by the raging flames and focused his mental energies on summoning Aghora and the Aghori God soon appeared his face as black as night, his eyes the color of the waning moon.

Adhanya unperturbed by the fearsome sight, requested that the Aghora unleash a plague that would consume the lives of all males and in return their widows would be throw alive into a blazing funeral pyre to which the Lord Preceptor readily agreed but he cautioned that should a maiden rise from the ashes of the cremation pyres then all would be lost.

The fueling of cremation pyres was a precondition to the Sects continued existence for Aghori magic is derived from the ashes of the funeral pyre. Thus far no one outside the Sect has been able to perform Aghori rites successfully and harness the rewards with the exception of me Amesha Spenta. It was an Aghori rite that I performed when I drove a dagger into the belly of my other half and ingested the remains from her pyre.

Adhanya smiled, it was highly improbably that a mortal maiden could resurrect herself from the ashes of a cremation pyre and thus he agreed.

As promised a plague soon swept through the Empire. It raged like an insatiable wildfire consuming the lives of men at an alarming rate. The plague weakened the defenses of the Empire considerably and the armies of Ahriman swooped on the villages and threw any widow they could get their hands on into the funeral pyres.

In the northern precincts of the Empire on the fringes of its northernmost border with the outlands, a female mendicant was doing her normal rounds begging for alms when she stumbled across a group of marauding soldiers on Adhanya's pay list.

Mistaking her for a widow, the men lifted her and threw her into a fire and laughed mockingly as the fire ate away at her flesh and watched as the skin was peeled away by the flame and the bones were roasted until they cracked to reveal the marrow within that quickly turned to liquid before it evaporated and vanished into thin air. It was at least an hour before the fire died down and the mendicant was reduced to ashes.

They turned towards their horses and just as they were about to clamber onto their rides they heard a noise behind them. They turned to look and they saw the ashes gather in a little heap. The soot and ashes from the pyre began to pile up until they slowly grew to the size of a small hill. Surprised the men stared opened mouth at the unusual spectacle before them. It took shape and betrayed the form of an old hag, bent and twisted clothed in a white sari, her hair tangled and uncombed, her skin wrinkled and decayed, sparkling with the black ash of the funeral pyre.

On her shoulder a black crow sat perched chewing on a piece of decayed flash. The hag grew in size and soon towered above the men who stood rooted to the grow, unable to move, their limbs frozen, as they grappled with fear.

She leaned over and bit the head off the first soldier, swallowing it with a single bite and devoured the rest of the men alive. As she munched on the bones a sharp fragment pierced her gum and a drop of her blood oozed out and fell to the ground.

It was instantly absorbed by the porous topsoil and soon made its way into the waterway, multiplying as it did so. It proved to be an antidote for the sickness and soon the plague that infested the Empire was brought to an end. The Goddesses name was Dhumawati and her Sect consists only of widows. She is worshiped by the shamans of the Betan Plateau for her ability to combat any illness but be warned, she is summoned only by blood sacrifice and often the blood that she requires is that of a mortal.

The Demons distraught from their failure summoned the help of Madan who was a Demon-sage of great prowess. After meditating upon Shiva for a thousand years he was granted a boon and the boon that he requested was to have all that he said come true. Thus having acquired the devastating boon he isolated himself on a distant ice filled planet, calcified and solidified by magic. The Demons with the help of Ahriman approached Madan for help and the wrathful Demon agreed.

Fortunately spies on the payroll of the Empire had uncovered the plot and while the Demons were preoccupied with the summoning of Madan, Vishvamitra sought the assistance of the Sect leaders.

It was crucial that Madan be stopped before he condemned the Grand Empire to a fate worse than death. The leaders of the Sects sifted through the warehouse that was the super-consciousness in search of answers and soon stumbled on the patron Goddess of the planet Alger,

Bagalamukhi who was gifted with the ability to stop speech or from putting thought to words by seizing the tongue of her victims.

Vishvamitra projected himself on to the planet through transcendental sleep and begged the benevolent Goddess for her assistance. The Goddess consented and just as Madan was to about to utter the words that would result in the destruction and annihilation of the mortal world, the Goddess intervened.

She appeared before him and as he opened his mouth to speak, she reached out with her hand and seized the Demon's tongue before slicing it off with her sword, thereby rendering the Demon speechless. She is worshiped by the shamans of the Betan Plateau for her ability to render her enemies speechless and therefore other shamans, magicians and priests are not able to repeat the mantras that might instigate or repel an attack. Likewise, members of her Sect are able to stop the speech or thought of their enemies and reduce them to a state of temporary paralysis which if allowed to continue would induce death.

The Demons having been unsuccessful at war, devised a plan to starve the mortal race into submission. They summoned the aid of the rot Demon Atahzirna who orchestrated with the aid of spores, that spread with the wind, a blight that would accelerate rot in fruits and vegetables.

Crops withered as soon as they were harvested and fresh food was no longer available in the land and soon mortals became ill and diseased as a result of consuming rotten food. Faced without an option the Sect leaders once again scoured the vast collective library and stumbled across a planet that was entirely polluted by waste.

The color of the sky was a jaded green. Moss and fungi thrived rampantly on the surface of the planet and were its only inhabitants or occupants. The growth provided the surface of the planet with a natural green carpet smitten with flashes of lively yellow. There seated on a throne was a Goddess young and pretty, her skin the white of snow, her features sharp and haughty. Tall, lean and slim she sat on a golden throne, on a planet devoid of vegetation.

Her name was Matangi, the Tantric Goddess who reverses the rot sequence. The Sect leaders appealed to her for her help and with her assistance successfully managed to reverse the effects of Atahzirna's black magic. In return the Sect of Matangi was allowed to flourish in the Empire and like their goddess they had the ability to reverse the effects not only of decay and pestilence but also of black magic. Matangi is worshiped and revered by the shamans of the Betan Plateau primarily for this reason.

In the ensuing war most of the magical creatures were almost wiped out. The black magic that originated from the Temple of Ahriman had polluted the air and thinned it. The effects of black magic negated the white magic which was a source of sustenance for all magical creatures and scores of these wonderful beings had been erased from existence.

They remained only in sanctuaries that were rife with white magic covered by a magical shield that prevented black magic from seeping through. Many however had also left for other planets where they were safe from the clutches of Adhanya, but no one was safe from Ahriman and as the clock ticked and the end of the universe drew closer, every planet in the universe would be embroiled in the conflict.

The intervention of the Tantric Goddesses had greatly weakened Adhanya and he was forced to withdraw his

Demonic forces back to the Central Kingdoms where the black magic in the air was firmly held in place by the vice like grip of Ahriman.

As the battle drew to a close the Vedic Sects summoned the aid of the tenth Tantric Goddess, the Goddess Kamala who epitomizes the beginning and the end. With her aid and assistance Adhanya's forces were evicted from the Grand Empire and the Empire started again.

The re-birth of the Grand Empire was blessed by Kamala and the duration of its existence was for the length of the old calendar. Kamala is worshiped by the Shamans of the Betan Plateau to put an end to old feuds and usher in new enmities. Shamanism has at is core rivalries and the conflict between white and black magic is essential to the survival of shamans.

Central to the worship of Tantric Goddesses, it the highest ranking Goddess in the Tantric echelon, the Goddess Varahi who was the Goddess Protector of the Demon Slayer Mägi and though it is rarely mentioned, the Goddess Varahi is the balance that holds the Tantric circle in equilibrium.

Dron is principally propitiation by means of incantation. It is shamanistic in believe, ritualistic in practice and paganistic in substance. It is the appeasement of spirits in return for their aid or assistance and in the process shamans though they have ascended the shaman tree sometimes require the assistance of the Tantric Goddesses.

Spirits exist at different levels and they are not all equal in strength. The longer the spirit remains on the mortal plane, it increases in stature and as it does so its abilities compound. Spirits consume the elixir of life, blood and the more spirits are fed the more they increase in strength. There are often situations where two shamans have to battle it out for supremacy. Under most circumstances the shaman that possess the stronger spirit will prevail unless of course he summons the aid and assistance of the Tantric Goddesses.

Dron has evolved to its present stature and it has become more acceptable with the passage of time following the intervention of Lord Mägi who relegated the spirits that once occupied the Plateau back to the nether regions but Dron in its initially stages wasn't merely the appeasement of spirits but the appeasement of Demons.

Central to Dron worship is the yungdrung, an eight armed cross which is the key to unlocking the door to the other world. It is a faith of communion with spirits or Demons, conjured or invoked for answers and solutions. The pivotal figure and the founder of the Dron faith is Gshen-Rab.

Gshen-Rab was born in the Betan Plateau at a time the Grand Empire was at its weakest and Hawk's Nest was too engrossed with matters in other parts of the Empire, its forces stretched to the limit and its resources restricted.

Unable to interceded or intervene they allowed the Dron faith to blossom or fester, depending on which side of the coin one is on. Gshen-Rab was the rightful prince of the Plateau and destined to be duly crowned with the consent of the Sect Leaders. He was a blessed child gifted with abundant quantities of the talent. He could see into the future and communicate with spirits. They were visible to him when no others could see them. At the tender age of twelve, he was abducted from his father's palace and spirited away under the cover of darkness by Demons to the nether regions and there he was inducted into the Dron faith.

He was taught the secrets of spirits and Demons by his captors and he proved to be a willing and able learner. He was tutored and mentored by the demon lords for twelve years. He returned to the mortal world at the age of twenty-four, his knowledge of the spirit world and the demon world complete and intact. Upon marriage and having been gifted with children, he shared his knowledge with his progeny and they became his earliest disciples.

In time the Demons who captured him, cohorts of Ahriman decided that it was time to install a Demon Lord on the throne of the Betan Plateau and the Demon Lord Samsara and his consort Mara were duly appointed but the Sect Leaders refused to intervene because Gshen-Rab was the rightful heir to the throne and the choice to abdicate was his.

More importantly however was the birth of the Demon Slayer Mägi whose birth had been foretold by the oracle of Akashwani. The Temple of Akashwani is located within the formidable walls of Hawk's Nest.

Despite the many texts that exist and the numerous Gods and Goddess, I fear that the vice-like grip that Hawk's Nest maintains on the religious order may slip and many of those who reside within the former Empire may resort to other means and mechanisms to quench their spiritual thirst and elevate their spiritual knowledge. Therefore, I have decided to divulge the secret of the ages in a manner or a method through which others may have access to the vast, unlimited knowledge that is stored in the collective consciousness or the super-consciousness.

Mandukya Upanishad I

'O salutations to Lord Indra, how fortunate we are to hear with our ears the blessed words of praise, benediction and devotion, in honor of the Lord of the Heavens. The words that bestow good fortune to all who hear it'

'May we see with our eyes the offerings made to him who is stolid and steadfast in his task, he who is of the race of excellence, he who is greater than any being possessing a soul or a spirit and he who is infinitive in his life and in his grace'

'Exalted from the beginning of time is Indra, he who has stood glorious in deeds and he who has been celebrated from the dawn of humanity. May he cherish us in his keep, nourish us with his blessings, shower us with his love and cover us with his glory'

'Blessings unto him and unto us. We call upon the mighty Garuda to protect us from all evil while we regress into transcendental slumber. We call upon Brishaspatir, teacher of the gods, to guide us and to preserve the knowledge that we acquire during our meditative sleep. Peace to all'

Before reading the contents of any of the sacred texts it is customary to invoke the blessings of the gods. The most appropriate God to summon during the invocation rite is

Indra, the Guardian of the Heavens and he who never fails to appear in each and every Manvantra.

There are in total thirty-three million gods and goddesses in the Vedas and accordingly there are thirty-three million Sects that occupy the universe in each universal cycle. Indra however remains constant and thus he is venerated first and foremost.

Indra first appeared in the mortal world when a serpent-eel chieftain (Tiamat) invaded it. He and his offspring held the waterways of the world captive, encircling streams, rivers, lakes and other watery expanses with their slimy, slithery bodies and in so doing starved the soil of water, inducing a severe drought as a result of which crops withered and the land turned dry and arid.

The sages who first inhabited the mortal world cried out in despair and pleaded with the positive aspect of the Brahmatma for their assistance and in response to their pleas, Vishnu, came down from the throne of heaven astride his white elephant Airavata, a mighty white mammoth, with tusks of ivory that could bring down the tallest citadel, dressed in his brazen armor that was as effulgent as the sun.

When he set foot on the world the mountains cowered in fright and the surface trembled in fear. He wrestled with the serpent-eels unleashing repeated bolts of lightning which stuck the eels in all parts of their bodies and forced the vile creatures to relinquish the firm grip that they had on the waterways of the world and the precious elixir once again flooded the streams and rivers.

Finally, he smote the sons of the serpent-eel chieftain with crackling thunderbolts and they all perished save one, Vrta, the mightiest of Tiamat's sons. Angered and bewildered by the death of its siblings, Vrta, challenged the mighty Indra to a duel. The Guardian of Heaven unleashed volts of fastidious thunderbolts and reduced the mightiest of the serpent-eels to a crust. It soon lay prostrate on the ground beaten, battered and lifeless.

Having disposed of its sons, Indra confronted the beast that had carried the infant Vrta and its siblings in its belly, Tiamat, and reduced it to a charred carcass with his fiery bolts of lightning. The prime serpent-eel was so large that its body covered entire continents and when its remains decomposed it furbished the surface of the mortal world with nutrients.

By virtue of slaying Tiamat and Vrta, Indra became the first dragon slayer and this feat would be repeated by my many others including Dragos, Lord Preceptor and Protector of the Dragon Race.

In accordance with Vedic traditions the rite of summoning or invocation requires an offering and these offerings are usually made at an altar which is rectangular in shape and filled with dried wood. A fire is lit to summon Agni, the most sapient of beings, the messenger of the gods, who ferries the offerings to the respective Gods. Offerings in the Vedic tradition do not contain meat or any substance or ingredients containing meat or meat extracts unless of course the offerings are magical, occult or Tantric in nature.

Once the fire is lit and the altar is fueled with ghee, offerings are made by casting selected items into the fire. These items include fruits, sandalwood, milk, honey and sugarcane.

Let me also elaborate briefly on Indra. He belongs to the race of Gods or the race of excellence as opposed to the race of mortals. They race of Gods is also sometimes referred to as the sons of Aditi or descendants of the Solar Dynasty or Devas. Indra is the lord of the Devas. The term "Deva" is used to denote all those who belong to the race of gods.

The primary reason that Indra is invoked before regressing into transcendental sleep or slipping into meditative sleep is to protect the sleeper when he or she crosses the hypothetical bridge that connects the subconscious mind to the super-consciousness from evil spirits that are constantly lurking around every dark and murky corner, ready and prepared to lead any person astray should he or she falter.

In addition to Indra the mighty bird of prey, Garuda, is also invoked to protect the sleeper from straying during the journey. To the Vedic Sects, the mighty bird of prey is a vengeful guardian who serves to protect and preserve the sanctity of Vedic teachings and therefore it is the most coveted guardian during all Vedic rites and ceremonies.

Lastly it is also pertinent and relevant to call upon Brishaspatir who occupies an exalted position in all Vedic Sects because he is the foremost teacher of the Devas. The contents of the texts that I'm about to divulge will lead all who follow it to a higher goal or purpose.

Brishaspatir will help those that call upon him realize the invaluable truths of the sacred texts which unlike contemporary texts that revolve around mantras and the worship of Gods and Goddesses, the sacred texts lead us directly to the to the super-soul or the super-consciousness.

Mandukya Upanishad II

'O praise to the sound of aum, the primordial sound, the eternal sound, the sound of creation, the sound of the universe, the sound of all things and the sound of nothing, the sound of the past, the present and the future. The sound that is indestructible and inexhaustible, the sound of the beginning and the end. We ask that our sins be washed away, that our bodies be purified and that we attain the knowledge that we so honestly and earnestly desire'

The first verse in the Mandukya Upanishad emphasizes the importance of the word aum. It is the most commonly used word during worship and it is paramount that we understand its significance. It is also important to distinguish between the word and the sound. A very common misconception is that the impact of a mantra or a verse is reliant on the words used. Nothing could be farther from the truth. The fabrics of the universe are held together by the reverberations that emanate from a specific sound. The universe as we know it is sound based and not text based. That is the first principle in achieving greater awareness of the Brahmatma or the super-consciousness.

Aum is the primordial sound that sends ripples of minute waves to every corner, nook and cranny of the universe. It is the sound of the universe and should one be fortunate enough to meld with the super-consciousness and in so doing achieve the ability to transgress the borders of space and time, they would realize that the prevalent sound during interstellar or cosmic travel is aum.

Let us picture ourselves drifting in limitless space and let us position ourselves in the void between two planets. In accordance with the laws of the conscious mind or the rational mind there shouldn't be a sound and the ears should only be filled with deafening silence but silence itself is a sound and as we continue to linger in the void between planets the sound of the universe will become increasingly more audible to our ears. The sound is condensed into three syllables i.e. aum.

Because of the effects and the impact of the sound pronunciation and enunciation are of paramount importance and the word aum will only have the desired effect if repeated with the correct intonations and the appropriate inflections. Therefore, merely repeating the word aum without the proper cadence will not eventuate or perpetuate the desired outcome.

The mortal world represents the threefold states of time. The first syllable in the word represents the conscious state or the state of awakening which is relevant to the conscious mind and the mortal body. The second syllable represents the dream state while is relevant to both the conscious mind and the subconscious mind and implicates both the physical body and the soul. The third syllable in the word represents the comatose, meditative or the transcendental state that is relevant to the subconscious mind and the soul. Therefore, we can easily surmise that the word aum is relevant to the three states of existence bearing in mind that death is not the end of existence, it is merely the migration of the soul from on state to another and the next state after death is divided into three categories the spirit state, the spiritual state and rebirth.

The spirit state is relevant to those who have perished before the preordained or predestined time and as mentioned earlier they can continue to remain as spirits and rise up the spirit hierarchy with the help of shamans and regular or routine sacrificial offerings.

The same spirit can also realize the positive aspects of the Brahmatma and continue to exist by evolving into a spiritual being that confers benefits upon those who seek its assistance. However, the requirement for sustenance remains.

Spirit help is invaluable to those who live in isolated locations for without access to the spiritual knowledge that we possess especially in terms of combating physical illnesses. Therefore shamans do serve a valuable purpose. It is at the end of the day a question of social utility.

Those that meet a timely demise or die at the predestined time, make the journey through to the kingdom of Yama there to be adjudged by the God of Death and once he has dispensed with the appropriate punishment and once the guilty or sinful soul has undergone the punishment that has been ascribed or prescribed, the soul is than reborn in another life. For those that have lived a life of righteousness they are reborn in a higher state of existence and for those that have led a sinful live, they are born in a lowly state sometimes as an animal. The most righteous of souls will attain moksha or liberty and liberty here simply means reunification with the Brahmatma.

That by no means suggests that all souls will be reincarnated for the duration of the universe or eight point six four-billion-year cycle. Most souls approximately ninety percent will return to the collective consciousness or the Brahmatma after spending a certain amount of time trapped in the birth and death cycle.

Moskha is nothing other then the unification or the reunification with the Brahmatma from which all things emanate and the sacred texts are designed to circumvent the mundane continuity of the birth-death cycles.

While many talk of liberation few realize what it actually means. Liberation is best defined as remaining in the transcendental state or in the meditative state for the duration of the universe i.e. to breach the space time continuum and to be at one with the Brahmatma and remain or exist without the constraints of owning a physical body.

Mandukya Upanishad III

'The super soul, the super consciousness that is the fourth dimension, the Brahmatma, is the absolute and singular truth. All things, everything, here and there, now and then, the past, the present and the future emanate from he who is the Brahmatma'

There is but one sole and singular truth in the entire universe and that is the existence of the super-consciousness or the super-soul and it is for all intense and purposes a dimension by itself, a dimension that is distinct and separate from ours, a dimension known only as the fourth dimension.

At a time when there is a proliferation of new teachings partly concocted by the disciples of Ahriman, purported to brings the Sects to their knees and to prolong the birth and death cycle, which is the ulterior or the interior motive of Ahriman, realizing the supreme truth will help all mortals escape the clutches of evil and hasten the journey towards achieving liberation.

All men are born equal in their first birth but because of their conduct they fall within the clutches of the negative aspect of the Brahmatma and in time lose all sight of the supreme truth. They find themselves trapped in a tangled web following which they sink lower and lower and reach a stage where the subconscious mind, the voice of the soul goes into complete abeyance.

By realizing the sole and singular truth the subconscious mind is regenerated or is reinvigorated and that in turn steers the ship that is the frail and fragile mortal body towards the Brahmatma. When the conscious mind realizes and acknowledges the supreme truth, all other things become trivial and irrelevant.

The journey towards realizing the potential of the subconscious mind and tapping into its vast unlimited resources is not without its fair share of trials and tribulations. The subconscious mind when it first enters the scene usually does so with a blast that takes the conscious mind by surprise and the images that flash before the mind are erratic yet rational. They are erratic in the sense that there is no conceivable explanation for the images yet the conscious mind has difficulty repudiating that these images exist. Despite being unable to make any sense of the images, the conscious mind accepts them as the truth and it is unable to resist the presence of the subconscious mind.

During the outer body experience which is a product of the subconscious mind the subject is flung millions if not billions of miles away from the body and sees things that it has difficulty explaining or understanding and often in the beginning stages at least the explanations that the conscious mind puts forward are wrong.

The conscious mind which is the rational mind likes to make sense of things and the process of making sense of things often involves only what the conscious mind knows. It tries to amalgamate the pieces of a puzzle, to get a clearer picture but the capacity of the conscious mind is limited to the picture board. The subconscious mind however harbors under no such delusions and merely projects images that it retrieves from the collective consciousness of the Brahmatma.

In the beginning nothing will make sense but as the subject acquires a greater understanding of the Brahmatma he or she will realize that the super-consciousness seeks only to teach and share its knowledge with everyone. Once the subject realizes this overbearing truth, it will relent and slowly acquire not only a greater understanding of the Brahmatma but it will also gain greater knowledge of the universe.

The knowledge that is made evident to the mind when it first comes into contact with the super-consciousness comes in inexplicable bursts and the images that flash before the mind of a subject, in a dreamlike state, flow in bits and pieces and it is pointless piecing information that appears senseless to the conscious mind and to do so would only lead to errors. Those who have opened the doors to the super-consciousness will understand in time that the information though correct may be misinterpreted or misconstrued.

At certain times the images or dreams that appear before the subject during sleep may be dreams of clairvoyance or dreams that foretell the future but even then it is best to wait for the event to unfold by taking no action with the exception of unfortunate events where it is advisable to take precautionary measures for example when the dream tells the subject not to go to a certain place then it is just best to refrain.

One of the biggest advantages of striving to be in close contact or in union with the fourth dimension is that some of these dreams will help us avoid the pitfalls of existence.

Mandukya Upanishad IV

'In the waking state, understanding the Vaishnarah (Vaisvanara), the strong arms that stolidly possess the consciousness (the conscious mind), is crucial. Realizing that the consciousness, is directed towards attaining material pleasures or desires through seven limbs and nineteen channels is imperative'

I have clearly distinguished between the conscious mind and the subconscious mind. The conscious mind belongs to the physical body and during the waking hours the conscious mind or literal mind (so called because it interprets all things in the most basic manner) maintains a firm grip on the body and it makes it impossible for the subconscious mind to break through. The understanding of this aspect of the mind is crucial in paving the way to unlocking the secrets of the subconscious mind.

The seven limbs (breath, head, eyes, mouth, torso, kidney / bowels / intestines) and the feet) are the seven conceptualizations of the conscious mind that perceives the whole as a singular entity that exists in unity and it recognizes that the singular entity comprises of numerous singular entities and both the singular entity and the smaller entities are governed by the principles of the five elements i.e. earth, wind, water, fire and space (aether). Therefore, the conscious mind perceives, the Vaisnavara, its understanding of God, as a single entity to which all things belong to and it acknowledges that even the smallest atom is in reality a fragment of the Vaisvanara and it mentally depicts God as an entity/being with seven limbs to facilitate its own understanding of God. It further acknowledges that the five elements are essential for continuity i.e. earth, wind, water, fire and space (aether). All the seven limbs are visible and tangible which is a compulsory prerequisite for the conscious mind and therefore the conscious mind cannot perceive God as something intangible or something it cannot visualize. In the waking state the conscious mind is preoccupied with the above presumption and refuses to move or budge from this notion.

The conscious mind having accepted the above as the sole or supreme truth then operates in nineteen different channels. The channels are the life forces (sometimes described as wind in shamanic circles) prana, apana, samana, udana, and vyana. The five senses, sight, sound, smell, taste and touch. The five actions precipitated by the senses i.e. seeing, hearing, smelling, tasting and touching and the four stimulants of the conscious i.e. mind imagination/creativity, longing/wanting/craving, ego/arrogance/pride and talent/wit/perception/reason.

In the waking state the role of the subconscious mind is temporarily suspended and the conscious mind which has control for as long as the soul is trapped within the body directs the body in the direction of the senses guided by reason and logic.

Mandukya Upanishad V

'The state where one falls into deep sleep is the stage the consciousness merges with the sub consciousness and the dual minds consolidate to become a single entity with the omniscient and omnipresent Brahmatma, un-fazed, untampered and unfettered by material desires'

The orthodox view is that the conscious mind and the subconscious mind are two separate entities i.e. the former belonging to the physical body and the latter to the soul. The Mandukya Upanishad expands on the principle and elaborates on the matter accordingly. When the conscious mind ceases all activity, the subconscious mind comes to the forefront of proceedings and assumes control of affairs. It is also possible to surmise that in order to realize the true potential of the subconscious mind and to build the bridge with the super-consciousness, the workings of the conscious mind or temporal mind has to first cease.

It is also possible to deduce that the temporal mind is solely secular in nature and it is preoccupied with materialistic or worldly pursuits while the subconscious mind is concerned solely with spiritual pursuits. To some degree it explains the contrasting impacts that both minds have and it is possible to surmise that the former like the body is temporary while the latter is eternal like the soul.

It is now relevant to look into the states during which the subconscious mind assumes control of things and relegates the conscious mind to the role of a mere observer.

The most common state is the dream state, a state where the conscious mind is aware and is able to interpret what flashes before the mind but it is unable to make sense of it or come to terms with it because most dreams make almost no sense and seem unrelated to the existence of the subject.

During the dream state the subconscious mind, freed from the shackles that bind it, triggers little bursts that flash before the mind.

Those who are blessed with repeated subconscious dreams are privy to divine knowledge and are made aware of the eternal secrets for it is said that the Gods themselves are present in these dreams but the conscious mind of the subject who has not yet realized the qualities of the super-soul, though it is able to decipher the content of the dreams, is unable to make sense or conceive or perceive the messages in the dreams and often the message gets lost in the interpretation.

Some therefore, not knowing the indications of prophetic dreams, and conceiving that they have something in common with human dreams, rarely obtain foreknowledge of futurity, and as a consequence of this doubt that dreams contain any truth.

Therefore, it is relevant and pertinent that posterity be made aware of the qualities of the super-consciousness and the qualities of the subconscious mind so he or she can accurately interpret the latent messages that the subconscious mind intents or purports to deliver.

We can also further surmise that mortal existence is twofold and dualistic in nature. One being in conjunction with the body and the other being separate and distinct from the body. When we are awake we employ, for the most part, the life which is common with the body, that which exists in conjunction and is dependent on logic and reasoning as opposed to intuition.

Subconscious dreams are filled with the essence and compounds of pure spiritual matter and sometimes an invisible or an incorporeal spirit surrounds the dreamer and the meaning can be perceived not by sight but also by other co-sensations and intelligence.

Sometimes a bright and tranquil light shines forth by which the sight of the eyes is detained and occasions them to become closed though they were before open.

There are times during subconscious dreams that the dreamer is compelled and propelled by an intimation that there is a presence, unexplainable, unintelligible and intangible in the vicinity of the dreamer and often the conscious mind is unable to make sense of the presence that avails itself to its senses and shrinks and cowers in fear.

Be at ease for what the senses perceive is nothing less that the presence of the Brahmatma but that presence can either stem from the positive aspect of the Brahmatma or from the negative personification of the super-soul.

Mandukya Upanishad VI

'The Brahmatma or the super-soul, the omniscient is the source of all things. Seeking or merging with the universal monarch is the path to final beatitude that ends the cycle of birth and death and brings about the demise of the karmic law of action and retribution. It is indeed the path for all living beings. The nine treasures and the eighteen super-natural powers of creation will avail itself to him whose inner mind merges with that of the super-soul'.

The Supreme Lord, the Brahmatma, the super-consciousness or the super-soul is immaculate and pure beyond reproach and its cosmic dimensions are beyond the comprehension of the frail and fragile conscious mind.

He is the source of all things and once an incarnate has successfully merged his mind with that of the super-consciousness, the nine treasures and eighteen super-natural powers (the power of siddhis) that all mortals desire to acquire will avail itself to him.

The nine treasures are precious metals, gemstones, exquisite food, adept in the use of arms, swords, daggers and other weaponry, clothes and accessories, trading in gold, trading in precious metals, mastery of fine arts and material wealth (all the types of wealth not aforementioned).

The eighteen supernatural powers are the eighteen powers belonging to siddhis. They are as follows: -

- ❖ The power to become small.
- ❖ The power to become large.
- ❖ The power to become heavy.
- ❖ The ability to become light (as in weight).
- ❖ The power to obtain any desired commodity.
- ❖ The power to read another's mind.
- ❖ The ability to fulfill personal desires.
- ❖ The ability to exert control over others.
- ❖ The ability to resist hunger and thirst.
- ❖ The ability to hear from vast distances.
- ❖ The ability to see over vast distances.
- ❖ The ability to travel with the mind.
- ❖ The ability to acquire the desired façade.
- ❖ The ability to enter another body (this could be an animate body or an inanimate object for all objects have a soul).
- ❖ To ability be born or perish in the desire manner (the universe itself is a continuous cycle of expansion and contraction).
- ❖ To ability be in the company of heavenly and spiritual beings.
- ❖ The ability to actuate and perpetuate contemplation.
- ❖ The ability to travel the breadth and span of the entire universe.

The sacred texts are not overly concern with worship and by following the methods prescribed in the sacred texts, even mortals can acquire the powers of Gods. It is pointless seeking god in temples, shrines and altars when the essence of God pre-exists in every mortal. That however does not suggest that mantras are not important. To the contrary they are just as important because they guide us in our journey to acquiring a greater understanding of the super-soul.

For example, at the start we invoked the help and assistance of Indra to help us in our pursuits and this is done because Indra is a divinity and therefore closer to the Brahmatma than most mortals, a beacon that shows the way.

Likewise, we invoked the help of the mighty Garuda and that is to protect us from the negative aspects of the super-soul that might guide us the wrong way for our purpose is to be united with the positive aspect of the super-soul or the super-consciousness and not the other.

As one goes into mind exploration through transcendental or meditative slumber, the ability to confront becomes increasingly important because the sleeper will see and experience not only the bright and shinning qualities of the Brahmatma but the sleeper will also come to envisage the darker side of existence.

The decision to be reborn or otherwise is in the hands of all mortals but a majority of those who have realized the super-consciousness will seek to reunite with the super-soul. This is done not to elude the miseries of mortal existence but because it offers an infinitely higher existence. That is the true measure of someone who comprehends the nature of the super-soul.

Birth and death is nothing more than a journey. We start the journey when we split from the super-soul to become an individual soul with a separate identity and we complete the journey when we re-unite with the super-soul and become one with the super-soul.

Mandukya Upanishad VII

'The state where one is in touch with the Brahmatma is a state where there is no consciousness on the inside and there is no consciousness on the outside. There is no inner nor outer awareness. The awareness is not frozen but it is neither aware nor unaware. It is neither visible, inductable, transactable, perceivable, nor comprehensible. It is a state that is un-definable and unquantifiable, neither tangible nor intangible, without character or quality. A state that is unthinkable. It is a state of perfect calmness. It is the state of purity and tranquility'

Having uncovered the existence of the Brahmatma it becomes relevant to try and grasp the physical qualities and the attributes of the of the minute quantity of the Brahmatma that exists in all things created i.e. the soul or the farvashi.

The qualities of the Brahmatma are concisely realized by comparing it to energy. Energy is a property that is converterable and transferable but it cannot be created or destroyed. Following the same line of thought we can come to the conclusion that the soul is energy and the physical body is matter. Energy itself like the Brahmatma remains undefined and yet it remains the single most important component or ingredient in the universe. It is the driver of all things.

Mandukya Upanishad VIII

'The soul is divided into three states comprising of the word aum, three different components based on three different syllables. Therefore, when we venerate the word aum, we venerate the three states of existence related to the soul'.

When we venerate the word aum we venerate the three states that the soul is in. Each alphabet represents a single state. The first state is the waking state, the state where the conscious mind has full control and the subconscious mind is in abeyance. This is the state that is least connected to the Brahmatma and the conscious mind has full control and is driven or propelled or compelled to fulfill the needs of the senses and satisfy its desires.

The second state is the dream state, a state where the conscious mind is least active and it is a state when the subconscious mind is free from the shackles that bind the inner mind and is somewhat free to roam but not without constraints because the conscious mind interjects and intervenes to try and make sense of things.

The third state is the state where the conscious mind completely ceases to participate or the state of deep sleep or hypnosis or paralysis, a state which can occur naturally or be induced, where the soul melds and merges with the

Brahmatma. It is also known as the meditative state or the transcendental state and the state where the super-consciousness fully avails itself to the subconscious mind. Mortals like sages can remain in this state for a very long time and most of them are more content to unravel the secrets of the universe. It is also called Yoga Nidra which is equivalent to meditative or transcendental sleep. This sleep can occur in various postures.

Mandukya Upanishad IX

'The omnipresent Brahmatma is the source and the cause of all things. He is the first and foremost of all things, and all things emanate from him who is the fourth dimension. He who acknowledges and understands this, acquires sacred and true knowledge, and becomes the leader of men'

Once the bridge with the super-consciousness is established and the link is cemented by mental energies, the knowledge that is transferred from the super-consciousness to the incarnate is limitless and many refuse to forsake their spiritual contemplations for mortal rewards but should they so desire, with the knowledge that they have uncovered, they will without doubt become leaders of men.

The knowledge that is stored in the super-consciousness is so wide and varied that it would take more than one lifetime for mortals to ingest the sum total of knowledge that is there and therefore it is not inconsistent nor unheard for sages to be in a meditative state or in the state of transcendental sleep for centuries.

Mandukya Upanishad X

'The Brahmatma or the super soul, shines brightly and passionately during meditative or transcendental sleep. He is the master of all mantras and has ownership of all knowledge. Therefore, to share the knowledge of the Brahmatma one must go into transcendental sleep or meditative sleep'

I have in my infinite wisdom decided that the proper course of action during these perilous times, fraught with danger, where the sanctity of our religious order is at stake, to harness the knowledge that is stored in the collective consciousness so that we may find ways and means, yet unknown to Ahriman to dispose of our enemies.

It is important that we acknowledge the importance of meditative or transcendental sleep for it is the only means through which we can build a permanent, long lasting and enduring bridge with the Brahmatma and to this effect I have had our engineers clear the caverns and tunnels located below the forbidden mountains and instructed them to construct suitable sleeping chambers.

I have assigned batches of those that are blessed with

exceptional quantities of the talent to disengage from all physical activity and regress into transcendental sleep to uncover the vast knowledge that is stored in the super-consciousness which is to be later condensed by our scribes and stored for posterity.

Mandukya Upanishad XI

'Once the Brahmatma is realized, in deep sleep, the atma or the soul merges to become one with the super soul, and shares a collective reality with the super consciousness, a state of paralysis that is neither conscious nor unconscious'

I have further simplified the journey from mortality to immortality, from the time we are born with our souls trapped in the mortal or physical body to the time the soul is completely freed and acquires or attains the super-natural powers that are attributed only to the Race of Gods.

We are all of the Race of Gods and we can all become Gods. It is only our conscious mind that prohibits or hampers us from acquiring the powers of Gods. It is the desire of those who belong in the higher echelons of Hawk's Nest, the Seventh Manu, who occupies the highest mantle in the religious order and myself who others refer to as the God King, to steer all those who belong to the various Sectarian orders in this direction.

Ahriman wishes to do the exact opposite and while we know the eventual outcome and that is the end of the universe and the rebirth we do not know as of yet which side would triumph for in the umpteen universes of the past the forces of light have not always been triumphant or victorious.

Thus far we have only discussed the single universe that which is occupied by the mortal race but the creative powers of the Brahmatma are not limited to the sole universe. In actuality there are many universes that exist simultaneously but the duration of each universe is limited to six point-eight-four billion years.

The universes exist side by side and there are transit points in each universe that allow entities from one universe to cross over to the other. The Draganos system for example is a transit point and Dragos, Lord Supreme and Overlord of the Dragon Race, is not of this universe.

Mandukya Upanishad XII

'Realizing that which is without name or syllable, that which is without form or substance, that which is pure, without duality and that which is in control of the cosmos is the sole purpose of existence. The word aum is the atma itself, which is the mind and the body, the singular entity that controls our destiny'.

It is important the we realize that the Brahmatma the collective soul is in shape and substance identical to the soul. All souls are but a minute and diminutive quantity of the Brahmatma.

By realizing the simple and far reaching truths that I have outlined above it is now possible for us to regress into meditative and transcendental sleep and merge with the super-consciousness.

Prologue

The Isha Upanishad or the Ishavasya Upanishad flows concurrently with the other sacred texts that I have divulged or will divulge and while they may be constrained in the textual content, the sacred texts are admittedly difficult to comprehend and they are more readily understood by those who comprehend the dualistic nature of the mind and the nexus between the mind and the super-consciousness or the super-soul. The sacred texts are in reality a declaration that there is only one Supreme Being and all else is but a representation of the Supreme Being who is infinite and limitless in capacity.

Isha Upanishad I

'Salutation to the word aum. That which is perfect, complete and absolute in this world. That which is all things and that which is nothing, that which is the beginning and the end, that which is the Brahmatha'

There is but one truth, above and beyond all truths and that is that all things begin and end with the Brahmatma. It a principle that those who embark on the route to salvation must acknowledge and understand and when we sail from the harbor towards the much sought after destination that is known as liberation the three syllabled word which is in reality, the sound of creation, will guide us in forging the nexus that we so desire.

If we seek to break away from the chains that bind us to the continuous and reoccurring cycle of birth and death it is crucial and essential that we comprehend and understand the nature of the all-encompassing soul that is in actuality the universe as it is and understand that by continuously repeating the word aum we lull ourselves into transcendental sleep which serves to suspend the workings of the conscious mind and opens the gates to the subconscious mind which initially floods our perceptions with images that sometimes make no sense and span the length and breadth of the universe.

Once the subconscious mind is awakened it is without limit and we find our minds gifted not only with the ability to travel through space but we also achieve the ability to travel through time. Those that have successfully melded with the Brahmatma will acquire the power of Siddhis. The word "Siddhi" itself denotes accomplishment, attainment and perfection.

To surmise, Siddhis acquire some of the powers of the Brahmatma that permits them to rise to a level of prominence. It is a fundamental principle of the Vedic Sects that all men can aspire to be Gods and can attain the powers associated with Gods. Anyone who is able to reach out and connect with the superior intellect of the Brahmatma will be able to do so.

Let us for a moment look at the powers attributed to some of these Siddhis and there is no better example than the eighteen immortals who are worshiped and venerated as Gods. Let us re-examine the mode in which they acquired their powers - to give us an understanding of what Siddhis are and to give us some understanding of the powers that they possess.

The eighteen immortals were not of the Sects but were in reality sages who had denounced Sectarian existence after realizing the singular truth. They regressed into transcendental sleep and their minds melded with the super-consciousness and as a result of the merger the acquired the gifts and the skills that they possessed. The eighteen Siddhis reside within the iron clad walls of Hawk's Nest but their exact whereabouts are known only to me the God King, Amesha Spenta, and the overlord Vaivasvata Manu.

The most famous of the Siddhis was Varnika who wrote the fate of all persons on scrolls. These scrolls include details of a mortal's previous life and Varnika was able to accurately predict rebirth cycles from the first cycle to the final cycle i.e. from the first birth to when the soul attains liberation. Varnika was a sage who lived the life of a hermit in conditions of extreme poverty and during his journey along the vast corridors of the super-consciousness, he stumbled across Brahma the creator, who divulged the fates of all members of the mortal race to him.

The second most prominent immortal is the sage Svarna. He is much revered among common folk and is often depicted with a bald head and a huge pot belly. A practitioner of herbal medicine, he was an alchemist with the ability to transform metals from their natural state to alloys or precious metals like gold - some with healing properties. It's a practice prevalent in many parts of the former empire and the transformed metals are either consumed or worn as trinkets on the body but it is imperative that these trinkets are constantly and consistently in contact with the skin. Proximity to the skin allows the healing properties within the metals to seep into the skin and cure the body of certain ailments.

Many of the transmutations contain plant and herbal extracts and it's the combination of plant extracts and metallic substances that create the undisclosed healing properties within the transformed metal. Svarna is also accredited with having discovered the alchemic process of transforming any known metal to gold.

The next among the great Siddhis is Tanu. He perfected the art of transcendental sleep and during his astral travels he witnessed the great battles between the race of Gods and the race of Demons. He narrated the sequence of events accordingly in books and scrolls that are stored in a secret vault in Hawk's Nest.

Tanu is followed by Dhrta who created the concept of Athistanam or prolonging life. The state of Athistanam is achieved through vibrations (mantras are important here because of the vibrations they produce) and repeating specific mantras will slow down the aging process or prolong youth. By following the methods prescribed by Dhrta the aging process of the physical body is stalled.

According to legend Dhrta lived for a period of four thousand three hundred years and spent many years in the Betan Plateau. Dhrta was instrumental in producing vibrations that altered not only the physical state of individuals but the nature of metals and the properties of base materials, like sand, gravel, gemstones, through the use of vibrations produced by sound.

The fifth sage in the circle of eighteen is Nibhtrartha. He was a mystic who delved deeply into the occult. His most noted contribution was condensing the principles of occultism into leather bound volumes.

True occultism or sane occultism has never sought to diminish the influence of faith. To the contrary occultism encourages religious believes because it is through religion and the resultant energies of love and devotion that the secrets of the subconscious mind can be unlocked or unearthed. The erosion of established religious practices and principles is not the work of true occult enthusiasts or anyone who displays a profound interest in the science.

White magic draws its energies from the positive aspect of the Brahmatma and black magic draws its energies from the negative aspect of the Brahmatma. The conflict between good and evil is in effect propagated to eventually bring about the end of the universal cycle to enable the next universal cycle to begin.

The sixth sage is Zlokakara who was known for composing prose and verses but he also had the ability to communicate mentally with others i.e. influence the thought process through subtle interjections via the subconscious mind. We have already established that the subconscious minds of all persons are linked via the super-consciousness and the only difference between sages and normal men is that the former have realized the power of the subconscious mind while the latter still labor under the influence of the conscious mind. Having attained the ability to tap into the super-consciousness, sages are now able to navigate through the labyrinth and access the thoughts of another person and therefore are able to make subtle hints that influence the decisions of another who has not yet acquired the ability or the skill to harness the potential of the subconscious mind.

Zlokakara is followed by the disciple of Varnika and Svarna who bequeath to their pupil the secrets of alchemy, Dhatuvijana. The science as propounded by Dhatuvijana is not only used to convert base metals to precious metals but it is also used to produce a combination of metal and herbal variants that are consumable. He further expounded on the teachings of Svarna. Dhatuvijana is regarded by mystics as the guardian and the keeper of alchemic sciences. The science of alchemy is deeply connected to the science of sound and the linguistic component is just as important or as equally important as the physical component.

The next sage in line is Vaidyaka who is regarded as the chief proponent of herbal medicine. He perfected many herbal cures and natural remedies and was credited with the discovery of the antiseptic properties of turmeric and the preservative properties of salt which he incorporated in his cures. Vaidyaka's concoctions are purely herbal and are derivatives of plants, vegetables and fruits, some of which are regarded as unpalatable in contemporary culinary circles.

Vaidyaka was also a skilled surgeon and far superior than any who existed during his time. He is widely regarded as the pioneer of medicine and facial surgery. All his surgeries were performed without anesthetics but despite the lack of pain suppressants his incisions and manipulations with or without surgical instruments were reported to have had a very high success rate.

The next sage is Manasvin and his contributions were in the field of mind control. His teachings enabled successful aspirants to control the mind with thought. The process starts with curbing the mind and restraining desires, a prerequisite to becoming a sage but mind control stretches far beyond that. It is essentially the ability to exert control over physical objects for example to move an object from one location to another and includes the ability to impose ones will over another.

It starts with unlocking the potential of the subconscious mind, which is followed by a melding or the merging of the subconscious mind with the super consciousness. It also corresponds with the abilities of those who have achieved the higher levels of Sadhana, literally translated meaning the ability to control and shape the mind and acquire the skill to exert influence over matter.

The next Siddha is Lehaka and he is probably the least known of the eighteen sages. He was a disciple of Varnika and Svarna and accordingly he chronicled their works in palm leave scrolls. He was a scholar of some note and he meticulously detailed the works of Varnika and Svarna.

Lehaka is followed by Kavitva Siddha. In addition to condensing the history of the Grand Empire into text, he is also a poet of some note and his contributions were mainly in the field of arts and literature.

Kavitva is followed by Dharmika Siddha and he is another sage connected deeply with the occult with the ability to make wishes come true, another common characteristic among all Siddhas. He is closely linked to the ten Tantric Goddesses.

Nandi Siddha comes after Dharmika and he takes his name after the white bull of heaven. He was a staunch devotee of the God with the matted dreadlocks. According to myth he was initiated by Lord Siva himself, and his expertise lies in the field of mysticism, occult, native medicine and alchemy. All occult sciences are attributed to Shiva and occultism is a common phenomenon among the Shiva Sects but they vary in levels of intensity.

Nandi is followed by Daizika Sittar. Two of his biggest contributions were the invention of the Kaya Kalpa techniques and the arrangement of the Navagraha (Nine Planets) in temples. "Kaya Kalpa" is a powerful technique that was discovered in ancient times and has been practiced in various ways since well before the age of Grand Empire. The practice has a three-fold objective: 1. to stall the aging process 2. to maintain youthfulness and physical health 3. to enhance longevity so that one may live to attain wisdom and spiritual fulfillment.

The practice of Kaya Kalpa confers significant spiritual as well as physical benefits because the mind and the body are energized and harmonized. This practice involves the restructuring process of the body in a natural way, so there are no medicines or herbs involved. Through regular implementation of this technique significant successes have been obtained in battling various types of chronic diseases and improving overall health and immunity. Kaya Kalpa is thus an anti-ageing technique that helps cure and prevent diseases and relieves many of the troubles that come with ageing."

Daizika is followed by Muni Siddha. As a point of interest all the Siddhas that we have mentioned have the word "muni" at the end of their name. The suffix connotes one of three stages, a sage, a person well-schooled in religious doctrines or someone who holds the power of the occult. The state of Sanyasi is a prerequisite to attaining the status of muni. In the case of the Siddhas the suffix denotes all three stages.

Muni was the Siddha who perfected inter-spherical travel. He was instrumental in forging formal alliances with genies and spent extensive time in their sphere. He formulated charts and navigational maps and has profound knowledge of the portals that open the door from one sphere to another. The word "muni" among other things also denotes "keeper of genies".

Nila comes after Muni Sittar and he was an alchemist, mystic, poet and an exponent and proponent of transcendental sleep. His exploits are outlined in a series of texts called the Nila Codex.

The next Siddha is the controversial Sarpa Siddha. He was a mystic who delved into the serpent realm and attained their powers. It is said that he has the ability to control the Nagas or Sarpas but because of his proximity to the Nagas or the Sarpas, it is impossible to determine his loyalties.

The last of the eighteen Siddhas is Jatakar Sittar who is closely associated with the mountain mendicant Shiva. He is the only person who knows the location of all the lingas in the universe. There are in total twelve Shiva lingas in the universe and these lingas collectively hold the power of Shiva.

Isha Upanishad II

'Osalutations to the supreme lord, he who is the cause of all things and all cosmic manifestations. He alone is the source of all things and therefore enjoy all that is given to you by him. Do not crave or desire someone else's wealth for there is only one source for everything and that is he who is omnipresent and omniscient'

The Brahmatma is the single source of all things and therefore he is the sole provider that man needs to seek in order to fulfill his spiritual or physical desires. In the context of the sacred texts existence is simplified by realizing the link with the Brahmatma.

As the battle with the dark forces of Ahriman continues, the forces of light will be confronted with hurdles and obstacles that at first may seem and appear to be insurmountable for those of us who haven't strengthen our link with the super-soul and thus it is imperative that we built the bridge as quickly as possible.

It is our only hope for victory in what will prove to be the most testing of times and will culminate in an epic battle. The end of the battle will signal the end of the Manvantra and the demise of the overlord, the Seventh Manu, Vaivasvata Manu.

Should we falter in our battle, the next Manu, Savarni Manu or overlord will be born in the Temple of Ahriman and I will be his arch nemesis. Six times have we fought and six times have we been successful but the outcome of the Seventh battle hangs in the balance and I fear that we may lose our way.

Isha Upanishad III

'To remain alive, to become a man or a woman, one must do the duties connected to or prescribed to him or her by the laws of karma. Only then will there be no stain or smear attached to him or her. If the laws of karma do not dictate or require a certain action to be performed, then that duty is not for him or her'

The Isha Upanishad further elaborates on the karmic cycle. I have briefly touched on it the Mandukya Upanishad. In most instances the soul starts out as a pure untainted component of the Brahmatma and becomes scarred and contaminated but is healed before it returns to the Brahmatma.

Existence is divided into two components, mortal life or physical life which endures for a short length of time or soulful life which endures for the length of the universe. Soulful life continues and even after death, for as long as the soul is encased in a mortal body, it continues to be driven by mortal cravings. Upon death the soul is trapped in the discarded flesh that clothes the bones until such time that it has journeyed to the court of Yama and the God of Death has meted out judgement in accordance with the conduct of the physical body when it was alive.

Once the sinful soul has atoned for its sins, the soul is reborn and at the time of its rebirth, Brahma pens down the fate of the new birth in the eternal book of fates which contains the fates of all mortals and the duties that are stipulated are related to the conduct of the physical body that the soul was trapped in during its previous birth.

While in the new body the soul is required to discharge its duties as stipulated in the book of fates and it will reacquaint itself with others who were close to the former body that it was entombed in. With spouses it is essential that they marry the same partner.

I have earlier mentioned in the Matsya Purana that the creative power of the Brahmatma divided itself into two separate entities one male (Svayambhuva Manu) and the other female (Shatarupa). All males descend from the former and all females from the latter and in order to have the perfect life it is essential to find the corresponding female half which is normally the case unless something goes drastically and dramatically wrong. Similarly, children are reunited with their parents and their spouses in the following births.

It is not compulsory or mandatory for the body or the soul to undertake or perform any duty or function that it is not required of it at the time of birth. In fact, it is the exact opposite and taking on additional responsibilities might accrue negative karma that will be carried forward to the next life. It is a lesson that I have learnt the hard way.

How exactly then does one know the duties that they are supposed to perform? The normal time honored method is to consult an astrologer with the date and time of birth but the more accurate mechanism is to consult the scrolls written by Varnika that are relevant to the particular person or individual.

Isha Upanishad IV

'The Demons, the sunless ones, know by name and have explicit knowledge of those who are destined to be great and they blind humanity, in their words and manner, to stop those that are chosen, from being great'

'The Demons, the sunless ones are those who are devoid of self-knowledge or those who are too enthralled with self-glorification or self-praise and therefore are unsuited to the higher path'

The Gods and the anti-Gods (Demons and rakshasas) collectively represent the powers of the Brahmatma. The former edify the positive aspects of the Brahmatma and the latter personify the negative aspects. The opposing forces are trapped in constant conflict but while the forces of light prefer an outright battle, the forces of darkness rather connive and conspire to achieve victory.

It is the purpose and design of evil to stop those that have been selected because of their positive attributes and contributions in their past life from becoming great, by leading them astray or by confusing and confounding their enemies through lies, deceit and other mechanisms available to the unholy and the unrighteous. Evil rears its ugly head in an unlikely manner in the most un-seeming places.

Isha Upanishad V

'He who is immobile or immovable, he who stands alone, he who is swifter that our mind, he is the Brahmatma or the supreme lord. He is without second, and he is first and foremost in all things. He is with or without form. He is the guiding light that shines on everything that glitters and he never ceases to enthrall. He is the sole possessor of the universe and the most benevolent of all beings. He moves like a breeze, swifter than light, and compassionately gives in charity'.

The Isha Upanishad gives some further insights to the nature of the Brahmatma and it is synonymous and analogues to souls that ascribe to the positive aspect of the Brahmatma. The soul is a tiny white light that is the size of a thumb and it is colorless and odorless, shaped like a little globe. It is this tiny white light that becomes active during transcendental sleep.

The most common transcendental activity occurs during deep-sleep when the conscious mind ceases and refrains from all activity. The subconscious mind is freed and is able to explore the vast library that is the super-consciousness while the body is in deep meditative or comatose sleep. There is realization and the conscious mind is able to see but it is unable to understand or make sense of what it sees and often the deductions of the conscious mind in the aftermath of transcendental sleep are wrong.

In the state of transcendentalism, the subconscious mind or the soulful mind can travel to any point in in the eight point six four-billion-year universe for it is in unison and is in one with the Brahmatma or the super-soul. Transcendentalism is reliant on the probability that the personality is divided into two components, physical and spiritual, i.e. the body and the soul and it is dependent on the soul being able to free itself from the body. Once this is achieved transcendentalism comes into play and things like astral projection and clairvoyance are simply bi-products of transcendentalism or the separation of the soul from the body. The soul achieves cognizance or realizes its potential and that includes its form, which is similar to the form of the Brahmatma.

The elements and the components or the ingredients all comprise of the one; they are held in their order by the one and when the mind accepts, and is satisfied with the one, then the consciousness becomes steady and stable.

All things are perceived and received if the one is obtained and the precious gift of human life becomes fruitful and meaningful. Without unity with the Brahmatma, all engagements and entanglements are worthless.

Isha Upanishad VI

'The Brahmatma is that which moves and that which does not move. It is that which is at a distance and that which is close by. It is that which is within, belonging internally to everyone. It is also that which is not within, that which is the exterior and therefore it is all things'

The soul once it is separated or is freed from the body during transcendental sleep, meditation or hypnosis has the ability to travel the length and breadth of the universe in the form described previously i.e. as a light the size of a thumb to any place or to any point from the beginning to the end of the eight point six four-billion-year universal cycle.

There are in our scriptures many cities and places that defy logic and appear to be improbable and impossible to contrive or conceive and it may sometimes come across as a figment of a someone's imagination.

However, most scholars fail to realize that our faith has to be looked at from the context of the universe and regardless of its incredulity what does not seem probable in the mortal world is highly possible in other worlds.

Sages during transcendental or meditative sleep were able to uncover the facts as they transpired by gaining access to the super-consciousness via the subconscious mind and are able to travel to the site of past battles via the precept of astral projection to garner or unearth the facts as they transpired.

We know that what they tell us occurred in the present universe but there is nothing to suggest that these events unfolded in the world that we occupy and many of the events that transpired occurred in different worlds and the conscious mind has tried to limit it to the context of the world it exists or subsists in and hence making it sound or come across as unbelievable.

Isha Upanishad VII

'But he who observes all things and all entities, he who thinks and discovers will notice that the Brahmatma or the super consciousness or the super soul exists in all things and thereafter he will cease to abhor'

Once a sage realizes the scope of the Brahmatma and the limitless potential of the super-consciousness and having achieved cognizance of time and space and the infinite yet finite nature of the universe, the concept of good and evil ceases to be of relevance or importance and it is replaced by the concept of duty, fidelity and loyalty.

The ultimate truth is that good and evil will negate each other and cause the contraction or the demise of the universe only to be reborn. Good and evil is of little significance but duty is of paramount importance and those sages who subscribe or are linked to the positive aspect of the Brahmatma will continue to be a part of the perpetual war against the negative aspect of the super-consciousness and the reverse may also be said for those who ascribe to the negative aspect of the Brahmatma.

While mortals make much of their suffering from the perspective of the cosmic being it is of little significance and the easiest method or manner to escape from the cycle of misery that existence often perpetuates, regardless of one's station or position in life, is to simply tap into the potential of the subconscious mind and realize the powers that lie therein.

There aren't many stipulations to follow and peace and tranquility by far are the easiest aspirations to achieve but it is hampered by the sensual desires of the conscious mind and that is the greatest flaw of mortality i.e. to give into the temptations of the conscious mind.

Instead try marveling at the concept of creation and destruction, the concept of birth, death and resurrection and we'd find that the problematic nature of existence is trivial. The soul or the furnace within the physical frame is the driver that propels the path to enlightenment.

The other common mistake that most of us make is to equate enlightenment with happiness which is not always the case. It is merely realization and recognition and there is nothing to suggest that the knowledge that is uncovered will make a person or an individual happy.

To the contrary the sage becomes cold and distant towards his fellow beings and the simple reason is because the purpose of existence is not happiness which can be equated to a feeling that one achieves when his or her desires are gratified. The purpose of existence is to seek knowledge.

The sacred texts are concerned with building a bridge with the Brahmatma and forging a nexus with the super-soul. He or she who has successfully built a bridge with the super-consciousness or the Brahmatma often relegates himself or herself to a position of being a mere observer and chooses in most instances to unravel the mysteries and the intricacies of creation.

Isha Upanishad VIII

'When one discovers, in silence and solitude, that all things come into existence from the super soul and that all things return to the cosmic soul, he or she is free from all grief, sorrow, bewilderment and confusion'

The realization of the ultimate truth or the cosmic truth will reveal that there is only one source to all things and being in contact with this source will liberate us from the cycle of birth and death and help us avoid the repressive nature of the all-pervading karmic cycle.

The cycle of birth and death has thus far only been limited to deeds, good and bad. A mortal is reborn depending on the nature of his or her deeds in a past existence but the cycle of birth and death itself can be controlled and one who has achieved the nexus with the Brahmatma can choose if he or she wishes to be reborn and to be reborn in a desired station.

However, liberation is the ultimate role or function of existence for at the end all souls will be liberated and reunited with the super-soul. The ultimate truth of existence is duty and one who has bridged the gap between the conscious mind and the super-consciousness through the bridge that is the subconscious mind realizes his or her duty/duties and will not falter in their task.

Isha Upanishad IX

'The Brahmatma is the all-pervading soul that is pure and white without estimation, without physical substance, without material faults, unperturbed by the senses, without limb and sinew, without evil or malice, wise and gifted with insight. It is the greatest of all saintly persons, pervading, guiding, surrounding and self-existent, in accordance with the truth - eternal and all encompassing'

The Brahmatma resembles the soul in many aspects and the soul that is trapped within the frail human body is an infinitesimally smaller version of the sum collective. The soul, the tiny white light, that drifts out the body with a mortal's last breath, is in every way identical to the all-encompassing Brahmatma.

Those who have remained pure and righteous during their lives and have lived their lives in accordance with the time honored traditions of the Sects are proprietors of white souls or souls that embody and reflect the qualities of the positive aspect or manifestation or incarnation of the righteous component of the Brahmatma.

Those whose lives have been corrupted and tainted by material pleasures and those who subscribe to the negative aspect of the Brahmatma are owners of black souls.

At death the soul is visible to some and for those who are gifted with soul-sight, they will be able to clearly distinguish between pure souls and tainted souls. Likewise, spirits that linger or choose to remain and ascend the spirit hierarchy, are divided into white spirits (the spirits proponents of white magic invoke or call upon) and black spirits (the spirits that confer rewards and benefits to proponents and exponents of black magic).

Isha Upanishad X

'Those who are blinded by illusion are destined to be shrouded in darkness. Those who worship in ignorance are destined to be shrouded in darkness. Those who are attached to ritualistic knowledge are destined to be shrouded in darkness'

It is now time to elaborate on the word Maya which in the language of the Gods means illusion. The mortal world is constantly and perpetually shrouded in illusion and it is improbable the any mortal will be able to distinguish between illusion and reality unless he or she has built the nexus or established the link with the super-consciousness.

All material pleasures are creations of illusions for they are not permanent and may disappear without notice within the blink of an eye or within a small space of time. Material pleasures are more tangible than corporeal rewards and therefore we cannot blame mortals for being deceived by illusion.

The conscious mind can only perceive and interpret what it sees and therefore its actions are very much dictated by sight. All the five senses play an important decisive role in determining the actions of the conscious mind. Maya or illusion avails itself to the sense and once this requirement is fulfilled or satisfied the conscious mind refuses to look any further, drowning out the thoughts of the subconscious mind with logic.

The projections of the conscious mind satisfy the logic and rationale test while the projections of the subconscious mind make no sense at all. The conscious mind seeks to make sense of all things and it can only interpret visible and tangible qualities. The conscious mind cannot make sense of intuition, clairvoyance etc. and the subtle suggestions and hints made by the subconscious mind often go to waste.

Isha Upanishad XI

'Thus we have heard that those who delight in devotion acquire knowledge from the Gods and Demigods, all of who are distinguished by the knowledge they possess or impart'

'Therefore each God or Demigod possesses different knowledge and is worshiped to acquire specific knowledge'

It is through the rite of worship that knowledge is acquired. Through the various rites prescribed by the specific Sects its members adopt the attributes, sometimes physical and at other times mental, of the Gods and Goddesses that they worship but the act of worship is in itself a path to reach out and establish a bond with the super-consciousness.

The established modes of worship prescribed by the various Sects are put in place for mortals not only to access the knowledge that their Gods have derived from the Brahmatma but to assume the traits, characteristics and qualities that are peculiar to them.

When I devised the sacred texts I sought to condense some of the knowledge that had been stored in the timeless vaults of Hawk's Nest and I hoped to shorted the journey through which mortals realize the super-consciousness and attain the abilities of their cherished and honored Gods. It was also to allow them the privilege of obtaining knowledge that is beyond the confines of the specific Sects through transcendental sleep or Yoga Nidra.

Devotion is a means to meld with the super-consciousness but it is not the sole and only means. The subtler yet infinitely more beneficial method is to build the bridge through the time honored mechanism of sleep.

Isha Upanishad XII

'Those who are able to distinguish between knowledge and illusion, by education, by worship or by transcendental sleep attain immortality after death'

The karmic cycle is governed entirely by illusion or material pleasures and all mortals are driven by the trivial needs of the sense and thus fail to grasp the higher fundamentals of existence. All is made available in abundance to those who realize the sole, fundamental and the ultimate truth and that is simply that all things are governed by the Brahmatma.

The Brahmatma is the father of all things, animate and inanimate and therefore he is the most benevolent of all things, pre-existing, existing or coming into existence, for that is all I can do to define the Brahmatma and despite being the God King, Amesha Spenta, even I cannot sufficiently explain that which is the Brahmatma and I am confined to admitting and acknowledging the fact that I am but a component of the Brahmatma gifted with more ability than others and blessed eternally by the Living Goddess.

I am her sword and I am her shield and it is me that she calls upon when the need arises. I am destined to, in all lifetimes, in all creations, in all universes and all spheres to battle the forces of evil.

The universe, each universe, all universes, exist in spheres or dimensions and the most well defined sphere or dimension is the astral dimension or the sphere that spirits travel to after death. Dimensions like parallel universes exist in the same space and time but are more accessible that parallel universes.

Like the astral dimension or the spirit world, the nether regions, hell, the underworld and the abyss exist concurrently in different spheres or dimensions.

Among the many dimensions or spheres that influence the mortal world is that of the genie. Genies are descendants of the Sage Kashyapa and his consort Muni. The genie is a creature that varies in size and it can appear to be as tiny as a fairy or a sparrow that fits into the palms of a mortal man or as large as a house or the tallest citadel.

Genies are similar to mortals in many ways with the exception of being able to outlive most mortals. Genies live for hundreds and thousands of years and the world of the Genie is almost identical to the world of mortals. They have kingdoms and they vary in status depending on their position and the houses they were born into.

Genies are powerless in their dimension but when they travel to the dimension of mortals they acquire immense powers including powers to grant and confer longevity, good health and great wealth. They are not classed as magical creatures because they exist in a dimension of their own, like spirits, and are unlike magical creatures that share the same sphere or dimension as mortals. Genies procreate like mortals and it is not unknown or unheard of for those who are well versed with black magic to spirit away an infant genie and rear it for purposes suited to their needs.

There are various types of genies that occupy the genie world. The most common genie is known as the djinn and it is classed as a worker genie in its world. However, like all genies when it is transported to the mortal world it acquires additional powers.

The djinn is the weakest of the genies and in its own world it is often relegated to performing menial tasks and cannot aspire to rise higher up in the hierarchy unlike spirits in the spirit world or the astral world. When the djinn is in the mortal world it normally occupies the form of a black cat.

Slightly above the djinn is the Nasnas and in its own world it is regarded as a supervisory genie and directs djinns. Mortal magicians who possess or own a Nasnas are gifted indeed because each Nasnas is in charge of a legion of djinns. These mortals are black magicians of the highest caliber or distinction, not unlike members of the Aghori Sect. If the truth be told it is not unheard of for Aghoris to have in their possession a Nasnas or two.

When we talk of inferior genies (djinns and nasnas) we talk of possession or ownership simply because once a black magician brings an inferior genie into the mortal world he or she becomes the owner of the genie and his or her soul, even upon death will remain in his or her body until he or she has handed the genie over to another owner. If he or she fails to do so, the rotting corpse may become a hapless carcass that is destined to roam the dark of the night in agony unless the genie itself decides to spare its master.

The next genie in the hierarchy is a Shiq which is above the Nasnas. Each Shiq commands a legion of Nasnas and it is often depicted as a deformed genie that is horrid and hideous to look at. It is summoned only by those who belong to the inner sanctum of the Temple of Ahriman. No mortal magician has yet acquired the ability to summon a Shiq but it is possible to communicate telepathically with Shiqs and receive guidance or instructions, an avenue that was exploited by Ahriman's generals during the battle before time.

Above the Shiq there are genies proper whose skin vary in color and is smooth and soft in texture. Some genies are of exquisite beauty and it is not unknown for mortals to copulate or procreate with genies. All genies have a will of their own and they connive and contrive to eventuate their personal designs.

The path of the genie is unknown even to masters of the black arts and they often falter and flounder during the journey. Djinns, nasnas and shiqs are collectively known as soldier genies and can and have been summoned by Ahriman in the past.

The first genie in the category of genie proper are Ifrits, with close ties to Ahriman's inner circle. Ifrits are willful and obstinate and with the exception of Ahriman, none can exert any type of pressure on them.

Ifrit females are regarded as the prettiest females among all genies and their beauty far surpasses that of mortal women. Warriors of Hawk's Nest have fallen captive to their charms in the past, and have deviated from their path, lured and enticed by a life of infinite pleasures.

The next category of genies are Janns or white genies that look favorable upon humans. They are summoned by white magicians for their aid and assistance and even among genies they stand out. Janns are shape shifters who can occupy the form of a mortal or an animal or even a divinity for the matter and often travel in disguise in the mortal plane and occupy arid and semi-arid areas.

During the formation of the Grand Empire Janns were instrumental in guiding engineers while building canals to facilitate the channeling of water. The mathematics of the genie is the mathematics of precision and it is with their help that engineers were able to construct rudimentary ducts to transport water to villages located in the driest corners and the farthest reaches of the empire.

Chief among the genies proper are Marids who are synonymous to warlocks. Marids have great magical powers that allow them to travel through time and space. Many are allies of Ahriman but it must be said that they rarely intervene in the affairs of the mortal world. They are known to be wish granting genies and can be benevolent at times. They can either prescribe to the positive aspects of the Brahmatma or subscribe to the negative aspect of the Brahmatma. Much depends on their constitution.

The hooded priests who belong to the inner sanctum of Hawk's Nest are white Marids, loyal only to me, Amesha Spenta. They are my eyes and ears. They are however fewer in number compared to black Marids and despite their vast resources, it is still necessary for me to maintain an extensive espionage network.

In addition to the categories of genies mentioned above, there is another category of genie that is summoned by those who belong to the Veetal Sect - the Palis. They are genies of breathtaking beauty.

When in the mortal world these genies require mortal blood to sustain themselves and in exchange for the gifts and rewards that they confer upon members of the Sect, these sultry, seductive vampires are allowed to satisfy their thirst for mortal blood by draining small amounts of blood when their victims are asleep.

Among the Vedic Sects there is a rare Sect comprising solely of shape-shifters who were created by the Brahmatma to suppress an uprising within a demon colony. They are known as the Vanaras or creatures that normally occupy the shape of a monkey.

It was the shape that they assumed when they were first transported to the mortal planet and offered shelter and sanctuary by Chandra Deva. They are gifted with the ability to assume any shape or form in the present universe that they wish.

The Vanaras Sect in addition to worshipping their chosen God and ensuring the continuity of their rites and rituals also commune with genies and are in constant contact with a species of genies called Elats.

Elats like the Vanaras are extremely clever and can assume any shape or form that they wish and are regarded as white genies or genies that avail themselves to white magic and are called upon by white magicians. The nexus between the Vanaras and the Elat is so overwhelming that it is impossible to distinguish one from the another.

There remaining genies can be divided into two categories, the wicked and the nefarious. The first are ghouls. Ghouls when they are in the mortal realm inhabit wastelands, marshes and graveyards. The feed off human flesh, often that of the dead, though it's not uncommon for a ghoul to bring about the demise of a mortal to satisfy its hunger.

Ghouls are avoided by both black and white magicians because they have a tendency to lure mortals to their grave in order to feed. They were initially brought over by one of the chief lieutenants of Ahriman who is a Syaitan – a genie in its own right to aid in his cause.

Syaitans are the kindred of Demons and they are malevolent and malicious in all aspects. They are pale, smooth skinned with two horns that protrude from either side of the head.

The ruling elite of the genie world are called Iblis or the genie kings. They are all powerful in the genie sphere and are gifted with occult providence. Even Ahriman has little to do with them. They are known to be friendly to mortals when it suits their purpose and they are known to be generous to their mortal worshippers.

Isha Upanishad XIII

'The face of truth, knowledge and liberation is covered with a golden pot (veil). For those who seek the truth, for the purpose of enlightenment, they need to first acquire the blessings of the sun, the remover of all obstacles.'

The sacred texts are designed for the forces of light to triumph over the forces of darkness and I feel that I have sufficiently explained the nexus between the both. I feel that I have adequately disseminated some of the knowledge that posterity may require in order to remain victorious or if need be, rebel against the forces of darkness.

I have to face the possibility that the eventuality may be an undesired outcome and should that be the case there is a probability that this text or a copy of it might make its way into the hands of mortals who are unschooled or are unknowledgeable in the ways of the Vedic Sects.

Should the fates conspire to bring about such dire consequences than it is my intention to direct the unknowledgeable to first worship the sun for the sun is the aspect of the Brahmatma that is the live giver.

The rays of the solar disc awaken the soul within all beings, mortal and divine, corporal and incorporeal, animate and inanimate. Its copious luster banishes all fear and doubt.

There is a possibility that there may be a time when our glorious and noble institution is no longer here and there may be a stage when we no longer are able to keep in touch with the knowledge of the ages that have been handed down to us by the Sects.

It is the will of Ahriman to eventuate such an outcome. Should the age of darkness dawn on mortality and if such an eventuality should come to pass then it is my intention to lead the mortal race in the right direction back to the source, the sun, which embodies all the positive aspects of the Brahmatma.

Isha Upanishad XIV

'Having indulged in the light of the glorious sun, I the ksatriya, see the supreme truth, in all its forms and manifestations and I understand that he or she who commands is the all auspicious one, the supreme soul, the Brahmatma who is the light of the spiritual world. The Brahmatma protects, safeguards, confers and withdraws all benefits. I take the reins of my flock, my group, my kingdom in a manner so that they may witness and observe the radiance and the glory of the supreme soul. I do this alone'

Once posterity has acknowledged the importance of worshipping the sun, they should choose among them someone who is from the line of Kshatriya's to lead them and to him will our benefactors pass or confer, after we lull him into transcendental sleep, the knowledge of the ages. The Kshatriya that is chosen will be an incarnation of the all enduring me, Amesha Spenta.

Isha Upanishad XV

'The bluish wind brings with it the nectar of material existence and the mind and the body are churned in delusion. The body or the transcendental body must venerate the primordial sound with will, might and resolution. Worship must be performed repeatedly and only then will the knowledge of the ages come streaming through'

Before I conclude, let me warn and caution posterity that the mortal world is filled with delusion and the benevolent and compassionate Goddess, the Great Devi Mahatmaya spares no one. To escape from being sucked into a tangled web, mortality after acknowledging the sun, must venerate the three syllabled word aum and lull themselves, in rectitude and solitude into transcendental sleep. Only then will the knowledge of the ages come streaming through.